More Low Life

Also by Jeffrey Bernard
in Pan Books:

Low Life

Jeffrey Bernard

More Low Life

selected by Andrew Cameron

Pan Books
London, Sydney and Auckland

First published 1989 by Pan Books Ltd,
Cavaye Place, London SW10 9PG
9 8 7 6 5 4 3 2 1

ISBN 0 330 31295 2

Phototypeset by Input Typesetting Ltd, London
Printed and bound in Great Britain by
Richard Clay Ltd, Bungay, Suffolk

Contents

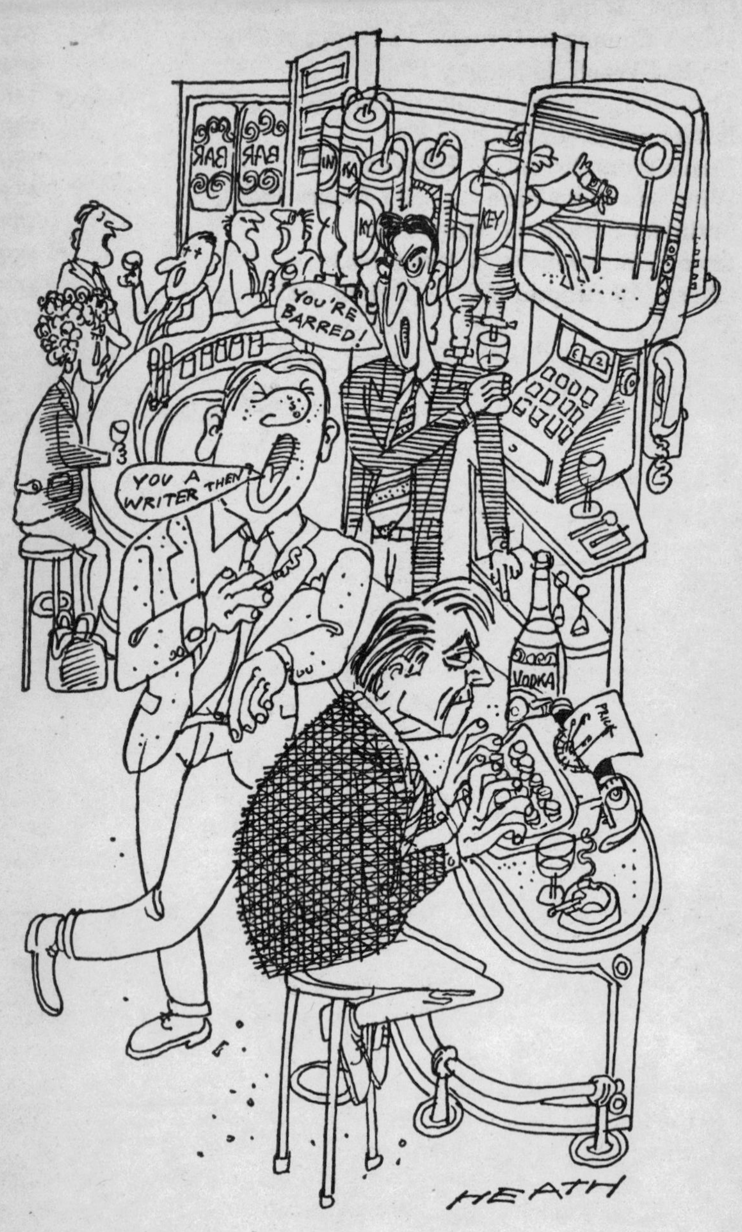
YOU'RE BARRED!
YOU A WRITER THEN
VODKA
HEATH

Preface by Beryl Bainbridge

What one requires of a responsible journal is that it should accurately document and comment upon current events. Prime Ministers' names are important, as are economic and political attitudes, but above all a voice is needed, one whose tone catches and reflects the mood of the times. It says much for the complexities of Thatcher's Britain that such a voice should belong to Jeffrey Bernard, although one has to be old enough to remember the England he represents.

On first reading one could mistake him for a man about town, a lounge lizard who spends his luncheon hours perched on a stool in the Coach and Horses struggling to recall the happenings of the night before. He has certain clues about his person; a lump of raw shish kebab nestling among the fluff of his blazer pocket, a paper clip mysteriously caught in his pubic hair, a bruise blossoming on the bone of his ankle. Like lightning, zigzag fragments of a former existence flash across his consciousness.

A man built like the incredible hulk had asked him to step outside and then proceeded to punch him to the pavement. Believing himself invited to stay with friends in the country he had appeared in a television programme 'starring' wee Georgie Best. The name Madeleine had come to him in the dark, first whispered, then shouted in poppy fields.

By tea-time, sat on a settee in a corner of the Groucho Club, he is struggling to forget. Fleetingly remorseful – someone called Tom nearly drowned doing a pooh in a river – he is unrepentant. Unlike Boswell, that other master of the low life, who, after falling by the wayside was always hell-bent on improvement, he is too wary of self-deception to pin his hopes to the tattered flag of his better nature. Besides, those forgotten bits had probably been enjoyable.

Sometimes he quits his native habitat and travels to outlandish quarters like Paris and Africa and Egypt. He goes because he's asked, and what else is there to do! He's appreciative and never less than informative, but abroad is a foreign land. It's true a man ought to travel, but timing is everything and possibly the jaunting has come too late. The world has shrunk, duplicated itself since the invention of the aeroplane.

Outside of Soho the only places he feels at home in are the Turf towns of Newbury and Lambourn and Newmarket. Perhaps he's not really a gambling man – it's the glossy animals he admires, the strutting jockeys, that 'huzzah' of the crowd as the horses race for the finish.

Each day heralds another battle for survival. His health is ropy and he's stalked by officials from the Inland Revenue and by VAT men. The Coach and Horses is full of deranged women weeping into the pages of the *Guardian*, and Norman's neck is infested with love bites.

He's temporarily without anywhere to live. Once he had a cottage in the country with roses nodding round the door. Now he's nodding over his typewriter in someone else's garden, baby-sitting pussy cats and furniture. Above his head, like the sword of Damocles, hangs the approaching deadline for his weekly column.

All the same, in spite of not owning property or conserving capital, of resolutely refusing to tell Syd about British Gas, of turning a deaf ear to the goody-goody opponents of smoking and drinking, Jeff speaks for the rest of us, those of us who pay lip-service to the way he conducts his life and yet who couldn't copy him if we tried. He both encourages our sense of anarchy and reinforces our erroneous belief that temperance in all things protects us from a fall.

On his part, I don't think it has anything to do with morality. He might join in if he could be bothered to study the form. One suspects he already knows that in order to win you have to nobble the rest of the field.

The point about good writing is that if it is to have any impact it has to swing between heaven and hell. It's got to be more than a distribution of correct words. There's a paragraph, one among many, in Jeff's latest collection of *Spectator* pieces which illustrates what I mean –

'In fact I've been awake all night thinking about it, bathed in the light from the wards of the genito-urinary hospital opposite my windows. I have been wondering about the inmates there as well. It strikes some sort of terror in me but it isn't so much the genitals that need love, care and concern as the mind and metaphorical heart. . . . It's so easy to avoid AIDS. A bottle of vodka a day will do it. A slower train to the same terminus.'

J. B. Priestley once complained that the very people he was writing for were unlikely to read him. But then, he wrote in an authoritarian tone of voice, sounding a ring of confidence few journalists today would dare to strike for fear of being thought pompous. These days, conviction is likely to get up people's noses.

It's an odd thought that the England which shaped Mrs Thatcher – give or take a few years and a difference in class – produced Jeff. They represent both sides of the coin. It should be noted that you can't have one without the other.

These are serious pieces. Forget the drinking, the hazy days and unremembered nights, the catalogue of medical indignities, those lost binoculars and mislaid overcoats. Actually, he doesn't need the binoculars. He can see into the distance better than any of us.

Beryl Bainbridge

Introduction

I was quite honestly a little surprised when Pan Books suggested another book of *Low Life* columns. After all, they have all appeared before, but since there was no work involved for me it seemed a good idea at the time. Now I am not so sure. Put together in a chunk they embarrass me. I can't bear to read them and I only wish I could write fiction. But the *Spectator*, like Soho, is a life-support system for me. A drip feed in weekly doses. There are people to thank for that. Mike Molloy, the ex-editor of the *Mirror* and then the *Sunday Mirror*, was the first man in Fleet Street to give me a leg up. In spite of some pretty appalling behaviour on my part he has been consistently kind. Then Geoffrey Wheatcroft who failed to get an autobiography out of me on behalf of Michael Joseph some years ago – who could – recruited me to write the television column for the *Spectator*. After a while, Alexander Chancellor noticed that I only reviewed old Hollywood movies that went out on Sunday evenings. I think I was in a pub or at the races for the rest of the week. That was discontinued and for a while I wrote a racing column. After about a year of that it was Simon Cortauld who came up with the idea of *Low Life*. It was Anthony Howard's father, a bishop I believe, who once asked him, 'Who's that low life correspondent of yours?' I had done some pieces for the *New Statesman* then. I told Simon and so the column came to be. Both he and Alexander were marvellous to work for. I got into tizzes and sulks on occasion and like Mike Molloy they were most tolerant. I began to realize that in writing for the *Spectator* I had joined a sort of club. Not a ship of fools but a ship nicely loaded with people with a highly defined sense of the absurd. My heart sank when Alexander left but since then Charles Moore has been an excellent boss. I have yet to abuse him. If I didn't completely loathe writing it would be a joy to work for the *Spectator*. (It would make for a better column too). Perhaps this book should have been dedicated to Molloy, Chancellor and Moore but Finola Morgan, She who would iron 14 shirts at a standing, has picked up the pieces between times beyond the call of any friend's duty. *Low Life* is, of course, a misnomer. I have no complaints and this is the way I choose to live. While Taki was languishing in prison I was steaming up the Mississippi and I have had a very good share of lobster, Royal Ascot, winnings, freebie trips, sunshine, champagne and whatever else it is that constitutes what some people think of as being the High Life. And my friends are 'nicer' too. They are caring but they don't care a lot. As long as what Beryl calls the 'sword of Damocles' still hangs overhead I suppose life will continue until the deadline. Loathsome word. As bad as the phrase that heralds the close of play, 'Time gentlemen, please'.

Jeffrey Bernard

More Low Life

Dear Ms Right

4 January 1986

Where were you when I needed you? I woke up this morning, reached out, and the bed was empty. Well, almost. There was a sock, a cigarette and a Wheeler's book match. But it is annoying the way you're so elusive. I've been looking for you now for 35 years and we keep missing each other. I catch glimpses of you from time to time, your legs disappearing round the corner, the back of your head on the top of a bus, but we never seem to come face to face. Perhaps you're not worth the search. What you are doing is clogging up the valley of what's left of this restless mind. Anyway, starting tomorrow we're finished. You can just go on living with your ghastly man. I bet he smokes a pipe and is in control of just about everything including you, his health and his dog. He wouldn't dream of taking a day off from shaving, never mind work, but what disgusts me most about him is that he is so bloody considerate. You know, *nice*. I'm sure he even smells nice.

What fun we could have had. You ironing my shirts and me pissing off to Newmarket for three days. And think of all those marvellous recriminations you've missed. You could have stabbed me in the back so very often over those awful woman to woman lunches you go in for. And you would have had the added bonus of feeling almost pious with your dreadful, liberal, broadminded tolerance. No, that would have worn a little thin after the honeymoon days. All right, I'll look for you for just one more day. The trouble is you won't be in the Coach and Horses because that's just a waste of time and mind, you won't be in the betting shop in Greek Street because that's just boring and silly. I don't know where you'll be. Yes, I do. You'll be in Selfridges buying buttons or curtain material. You really have got a hell of a nerve calling yourself Ms Right.

I can't bear the way you sip lager and I positively hate the way you cross your legs so neatly and respectably. Come to think of it, I'm damned if I know why I love you. After all, it's not as though you've got the looks of Edna O'Brien or the mind of Joanna Lumley. You are so ordinary. So why then am I besotted with you? I suppose it's because you're unobtainable. Are you forbidden fruit? If so, kindly learn how to be a windfall.

I grant you that it's pretty silly to sit down and write you or myself a letter, but I suppose that that is what it's come to. You see, secretly, and it's no longer a secret now, I think I'd like to be like you. I can't tell you how awful it is to be a man. People expect all sorts of things of you if you're a chap. Oh, lucky chapettes. People expect me to 'pull myself together'. People expect the man from Woolwich to regale them with strange tales of homosexual happenings in non-smoking compartments on the train to Charing Cross. They want Lester to win every race. They expect Francis Bacon to dazzle them with eccentricity every time they meet him. Above all they expect one to be a barrel of laughs. Sometimes I wake up in the morning and I genuinely go in search of old ladies to help across the street or children to rescue from burning houses but, somehow, I don't seem to get much further than the Coach and Horses, unless, of course, there's racing at Newbury.

No wonder we've never met. You've got to put yourself about a bit, haven't you? I'm in a rut of my own making. (Why do they call it rutting?) Anyway, I 'must close now', as my aunt from Clacton used to say at the end of her letters, because it's 11 a.m. and the bolts are sliding back all over England. Now, the sound effect of that is one Desert Island disc I would like to have.

But if perchance you happen to be about to have a tooth out and reading this auspicious journal in a waiting-room please contact me at these offices with a view to friendship and possibly marriage. I missed you the last four times. Actually, you can forget the friendship bit. That's asking too much. Let's just settle for wild, mad, abandoned love. Meanwhile, I hope you had a Happy Christmas while, at the same time, quite loathing you for leaving me here all alone to watch *The Magnificent Seven* and the Choir of King's College Chapel for the twentieth time. Oh, and a Prosperous New Year, damn you.

A Little Bit of Leisure

11 January 1986

Well, I did end up spending Christmas in the Middlesex Hospital after all. I was in a bed wedged between an ex-colonel in the paratroops suffering from circulatory troubles and cirrhosis, and an ancient labourer who kept mumbling that he devoutly wished that Mrs Thatcher and her gang would 'choke on their bleedin' Christmas puddin' '. I had forgotten just how much people are 'into' Christmas. The nurses, who made a point of not offering me a drink on the day itself, adored it, as did the visitors at their bedside parties and all the patients except for the colonel and myself – two miserable bastards. I sneaked the colonel a glass of dry sherry that had been left over on Sister's desk and drank 25 cups of tea myself. A respiratory consultant carved the turkey and two nurses took it in turns to dress up as Father Christmas and nearly died giggling. We all got a present from the hospital. Mine was talcum powder and soap which was all right after some cold sweats. They let me out on Boxing Day and told me that the time had come where I could no longer depend on my amazing powers of recovery.

But why is the Government ruining this excellent hospital, one of the best in England? The casualty department has closed down and the consultants have been scattered to the winds no longer having their own wards so that all is a little disjointed. It seems that Mrs Thatcher's attitude to the sick is now as it is to the poor. It's one thing for people like me with self-inflicted illnesses, but it's going to be awful for the unfortunates who can't help themselves in Mrs Thatcher's book. The Health Service is crumbling rapidly. Is Christian Science about to make a come-back? I hope not. Having been brought up as one for a while was bad enough, but just having read an extraordinary essay on the business by Mark Twain, 'Christian Science and the Book of Mrs Eddy', it seems even madder. A religion for the rich this one, so I suppose Mrs Thatcher approves.

And, speaking of being rich, I am on the verge of being so

by my own small-thinking standards. Since I have been back at home I have been bombarded by the credit-card people with written offers to lend me anything between £300 and £5,000. Am I mad enough to steam in for a loan, I wonder, before Gaddafi drops the bomb or the pancreas packs up? One final, carefree, mad holiday and splurge in the sun. It's tempting. But there's a sinister note in their offer. They say that I can use the loan for almost anything including home improvements, home appliances, stereo systems, sports and leisure equipment and weddings. And what are these synonyms for? Why, wives of course. I was once married to a mono system and I think I'm old enough to handle a stereo one now. As a matter of fact I spoke to her yesterday – listened to her that is – and the needle is still in the same groove. But it is the wedding that tempts me most, especially if the bride is sports and leisure equipment. I love weddings. Hope is such a wonderful feeling although I've always gone to the registrar's desk knowing I'd have to foot the bill for the lunch and then pretend I'd changed and settled down for a fortnight or so. The trouble is that out of four wives I've twice thought I'd married a piece of sports and leisure equipment only to discover that I'd married a home improvement. In fact after the honeymoons were over I went two months without any conversation because they were busy making curtains.

Another nasty home improvement I once came across was the business of not having a drink until the sun was over the yard-arm – she was a skipper's daughter. If I had had enough time there would have been a way round that. I heard an amazing case of a man who was confronted by the very same problem when he first got married to his awful well-wisher. (They do mean well, you see.) He lived in Kenya and when she first mentioned the nonsense about the angle of the sun and drinking he promptly planted a whole row of poplars in front of the house. Thanks to the climate they grew pretty quickly to cast their shadows but I don't think I could wait that long. I suppose if you married a domineering midget you could just plant dandelions or something. We shall see. With £5,000 in my bin I'm bound to get a little bit of leisure equipment.

Same Old Story

18 January 1986

I wasn't going to and didn't want to write a word this week. Nothing ever happens. *You* get up and go to work and probably do all sorts of useful things. I get up and potter about. It's quite appalling. This morning I went upstairs and had a cup of tea with my neighbour Jenny. We talked filth for about half an hour and then I went to the off-licence to get a can of beer and I don't even like beer. What next? Oh yes, I stared at a photograph of my last wife for an age and then put a cigarette out in an old cup of tea. Then I had to telephone a couple of pubs to find out where I had left my extremely expensive overcoat last night. It turned up. Then I opened the post – I have suddenly become strangely fearless of buff envelopes with windows – and one of my brothers had sent me a book of Hazlitt's, *Liber Amoris*, and his daughter had sent me a postcard with a picture of Byron. She is taking the mickey because she teases me about loving that man. So you see, it's not a very jolly start to the day. Had I still been married I could have had a wonderful breakfast overtured by an accusation about yesterday, with a slow movement, and a concerto for knife scraping burnt toast. God, how I miss the misery of living with someone. Actually I do live with someone. I have a bust of Nelson on my window-sill. He looks so damned nice it's awful. What else? Yes, I got a letter from a magazine asking me to write a piece about what women should know about men. Well, I don't know, what should they know? We get up, go to the off-licence for cigarettes and beer and then stare at pictures of our ex-wives. And we lie and scheme in order to remove their restrictive clothing. Then we cry quite a lot on the quiet, and having dried our eyes we look into the mirror and tell ourselves that we're really not that bad. Quite frankly it makes me want to vomit. If I had half the nerve I think I've got after a couple of vodkas I would jump over Nelson and out of the window into Great Portland Street 40 feet below. Another thing that got up my nose this morning was to realize that I actually fancied Jenny's daughter, Isabel.

She is 22. How can an apparently sane man of 53 possibly fancy a girl of 22? I must be going through the change of life.

But, as I say, nothing ever happens here. Take the situation to my left-hand side. There's this cup of tea that I've dropped a dog-end into, a telephone which has just rung from this journal asking why I am late with the miserable copy, an ashtray with an apple core in it, a plastic shoehorn nicked from an American hotel, and a bill from an insurance broker who was gambler enough to insure me against ill-health the last time I went abroad. On the floor is a copy of *Punch*. I write a column for them nowadays called 'Jeffrey Bernard on Women'. What I know about women could be put inside the head of an ant. It's very odd that. People quite frequently ask me to write about women and it may be simply because I have been utter disaster to them. What's awful about that is that it doesn't stop you liking them a lot. It isn't really all that sensible to like them if you haven't got boot laces to pull yourself up by. But there you are. Just above Nelson's bust I can see that secretary across the street in her office and my hours of idle speculation about her are fruitless but compulsive.

The other thing that bugs me somewhat today is the business of being asked to write about racing. If you had a label you wouldn't like it. Apart from my unhealthy interest in women I went racing first in 1949. I also got pissed that year for the first time. Since then, they all assume that that is all one knows about. Not so. I have seen flowers grow, babies laugh, kindness and love. Even so, here I am lumbered at this desk covered in cigarette ends and dirty glasses struggling to say something new about women and racehorses. Both are unpredictable, untrustworthy and utterly beautiful, but that doesn't really stretch to 2,000 words. You need to be a poet and that occupation doesn't do you a lot of good. My brother Oliver is a poet and he doesn't know the difference between Red Rum and Rita Hayworth. I don't expect P. J. Kavanagh does either but they come over well and don't spend their mornings gazing at Nelson's bust or the secretary's across the street.

Badge of Suffering *1 March 1986*

A young American arrived in the Coach and Horses last Monday to seek me out. He had been given my name and address by the girl I sailed up the Mississippi with two years ago. He turned out to be an egghead concerned with magnetic fields and curing people of everything from sloth to cancer by rearranging the said fields and making our auras positively shimmer with bright blue. I expect strange things from Americans but this nut introduced himself and then said. 'You write for the *Psychic News*, don't you?' I told him I didn't and held out very little hope for much entertainment after death which is why I don't want to die and which is why I was holding on to the bar with such tenacity. Me and my circle played the host to him for a pretty daft 30 minutes and then Sandy Fawkes said it. What we'd all been thinking. 'Are you one of those Americans who never buy a drink?' she asked. Bang on. There's a lot of them about and although the 'round' system of buying drinks has its drawbacks – it can make you drink more than you need to or want to and it can be financially painful when you're skint in a big group – it is nevertheless a friendly gesture more suitable and more rewarding than sticking your tongue down someone's throat in a public place. American hospitality stops beyond the American front door. But if you like someone or are simply with them conversing on licensed premises then you surely offer them a lousy drink. But why are Americans so serious? They are very, very good at making other people laugh but they have no sense of humour themselves.

The other thing that happened on Monday, an un-American activity, was that Norman turned up behind the bar wearing a brace around his neck. His constant peering into the till and at the cash roll has irrevocably damaged his neck but it is claimed by some that the brace is there to hide his love bites. Norman is 6ft 3in and his lady is 5ft nothing. It would require a civil engineer and a ton of Spanish fly to get her up there. Could anyone say of Norman, 'Why did you kiss him?' and be answered, 'Because he was there'? I think not. But he loves the brace just as small boys like to have an arm in a sling. We all have and wear badges. Show me a woman wearing red patent leather stiletto-heeled shoes and I'll show you a racing certainty. Norman's brace is a public statement to the effect that he has suffered and is still suffering. In fact Norman suffers from quite a few things that can't be cured by altering the magnetic fields that surround his incredible body. Apart from love bites and the scratch marks inflicted on him by women who have tried to rip through the thin silk of his Marks & Spencer shirts, there is his mother – Jewish just like Norman – VAT, lack of customers or too many badly behaved ones and several healthy, living relatives who stand between him and his vast inheritance. It was the air of almost autumnal melancholy created by the neck brace which made it virtually impossible for him to stare full-bloodedly at a girl who walked in on Tuesday that drove me to another watering hole, Groucho's Club.

I fear this place may well catch on and so get ruined as restaurants used to when given a good write-up by Michael Parkinson or Fay Maschler. A good reputation so often results in complacency. It would be nice if food writers could keep a secret. Not that Groucho's has had many write-ups, it has more of a word-of-mouth reputation. It is full of witty women whose beauty is generally so staggering you don't even hear the gems of wit that fall on the place beneath, the twice blessed bar. But there's a dodgy element creeping in. I saw two young men with their feet on the velvet-covered sofas. When I complained about the way young people behave like that to She who can iron 14 shirts, She said that they have always behaved like that. Not so. If I had put my shoed feet on a sofa when I was young my mother would have broken both my kneecaps with the crowbar she used to keep the servants in order. Also, young people who come to stay never ever think of replacing anything. They plunder kitchens like bandits. And yet another worrying thing I think about is has Norman got the brace around the right place?

A Soho Character

8 March 1986

A couple of Sundays ago I was watching *Songs of Praise*, which was coming from Maidstone Prison of all places, when to my amazement I spotted a man in the congregation of the chapel who owes me £50. He was standing there and had the gall to be singing 'Abide With Me'. I know that none of us are beyond redemption, although the vicar of Chaddleworth in Berkshire once told me that he thought I was, but I thought it was a bit of a bloody nerve in a strange way. It further struck me that he was probably a 'trusty', in which case all I can say is that the prison governor had better hang on to his wallet if he happens to interview Jimmy. I wouldn't swear to it but when it came to the last line of the chorus, 'Lord with me abide', I think Jimmy was singing, 'I'll take you for a ride'. I would have gone out to a restaurant that evening too if I'd had an extra 50 quid. Oh well, you can't win 'em all, and that, I'm afraid, reminds me that yet another of our Soho mates, Frank Blake, died last week.

The fact that someone is 74, smokes 60 cigarettes a day and drinks doesn't alter the fact that it's sad when a man dies. You want them to hang on for a little longer. Frank was a man who happened to be a terrible nuisance in a way with his nonsenses about being what he called a 'Soho character'. Nevertheless he made a sort of benign impact on the place. His family were a strange mixture. He was a fairly rough-sounding cockney with a fighting background and yet his brother was a Jesuit priest in Farm Street. Frank was best known as a master of ceremonies at wrestling fights and was often seen on television in that capacity. We first got to know each other years ago when I was navvying and laying the foundations of Kemble House, the block of flats opposite the French pub. Near the end of every week, penniless, I'd go up to his appalling flat in Old Compton Street and pawn something with him, usually a fountain pen, to raise 10 shillings. He loved it. It made him feel like something out of Charles Dickens.

The flat was quite something. It stands at the top of 72 steps and that might have helped kill him. It was a snip at about £2 a week, but, as I say, it was pretty ropy. He had to boil a kettle to wash or shave. He had a pay-phone on the wall along with a photograph of himself shaking hands with the Duke of Edinburgh at some fight function and he had a laugh that could have stemmed from a hysterical dog. We spent many hours in the old snooker club in Frith Street where Bunny May swept all before him at snooker and Frank would play kaluki, a form of rummy, with an assorted bunch of villains. In his more recent days he would bemoan, along with a lot of us, the decline of Soho. He would stop me in the street and with the face of someone who was lost would say, 'But where have all the characters gone?' He seemed quite bewildered at what time, the declining quality of life and Lord Wolfenden's wretched report had done to his little village. He used to appear in the Pâtisserie Valérie, above which he lived, every morning to get two bread rolls. The appearances were made in pyjamas covered by a pretty disgusting raincoat. And he always wore bedroom slippers. What he should have done was to have a more comfortable life. He had the money to get a flat with running hot water, he collected sovereigns which became devalued, but he was glued to Soho, a fairly common but chronic attachment some of us have formed. There is no known cure for it except for the road to Golders Green.

Well, there's not many of us left. I was totting up deaths and obituaries the other day and it is rather depressing but inevitable I suppose once you hit 50. It isn't Soho characters I miss so much as contemporaries. You find yourself looking around and wondering who's next. You avoid the looking glass except for necessities. One of the ways in which I shall miss Frank is that such people are a 'connection'. Not just to life as one is used to it, but to the past and simply being. Frank's biggest laugh was when I, desperate for £8, sparred a couple of rounds with Sandy Saddler, the featherweight champion of the world, and got damn nigh killed. I can hear that laugh now. It is a terrible sound.

Deep in Domesticity *5 April 1986*

I can't for the life of me understand why some people are so hell bent on stopping others from doing what they want to do. If I choose to close up my arteries with nicotine and then open them up again with vodka that is my business and I will. But apart from ASH there is now an organization called Action on Alcohol Abuse which is worried about the fact that 25,000 people die from drinking every year. What else should they die from? Eating? I really would like to be left alone by organizations. AAA also says that 50 per cent of domestic murders are committed by people when they are drunk. Well, of course they are. The other 50 per cent are probably committed by supporters of AAA. You don't have to be drunk to behave like a pig.

And I know about domestic murder. I lived with a girl once who tried to murder me. She used to burn the toast, insist on following me to the races and she was very much into sighing. You know, deep heavy sighs that make you wonder just what the hell you've done. The Guilt Machine I used to call her. She once even came to the Coach and Horses and stood in the doorway looking reproachfully at me. She didn't come inside, she just stood there and dabbed an eye with a handkerchief. She had another sort of sigh as well, much shorter and harder. That was the aggressive sigh and a nasty noise it was too. Such a terrible waste of a lovely body. Whoever it is who is responsible for putting the right brains into the right bodies really screws up sometimes. She was a dancer and I've noticed that dancers tend to be a little daft. I mean it's a funny thing to do, isn't it? I don't think it's *natural*. If you were with someone and they suddenly got up on their points, flung their arms in the air and then began to tiptoe through the tulips you'd send for a doctor or throw a bucket of cold water over them, wouldn't you? But this girl used to do her barre exercises at the ironing board. 'Just iron the bloody shirt,' I'd say and she would with a tremendous sigh. Well, she had to go and she did. She got a job dancing in Beirut.

Another attempt was made on my life by a girl who would

keep telling me how very wonderful her ex-boyfriend was. Such romancing. She made him sound like St George gone to work for an advertising agency. And yet there is no organization bent on saving us from being bored to death. It so happens that neither of those two women would have been so boring if they had taken the odd swig from the ubiquitous bottle. I sometimes wonder, now that I'm an ex, if she tells her current chap how wonderful I was. Probably not. I threw her too many wintry smiles to make her drop her gaze. It's surprising how nasty you can make a smile if you want to. I got so good at it eventually that I could look her in the eye and make her look at the floor in five seconds. So I don't think she is referring to me as Mister Wonderful at the moment.

Which reminds me. Something rather odd. I got chatting with a bloke in a pub the other day and I'd never met him before. One thing led to another and he started telling me about his girlfriend's ex-boyfriend. After a minute or two it dawned on me that he was talking about me. I sounded really awful, from smoking in bed first thing in the morning to disappearing to Newmarket for a week with all the housekeeping money. Of course I was fascinated and I led this bloke on getting more and more information about me. Apparently, apart from smoking, racing and drinking, I have an ungovernable temper, fall asleep in restaurants or eat Indian takeaways in bed, snore and wear the same polo-neck jersey for days on end. Well, it's news to me although I must admit I did once wake up one morning to find some curry in one of my shoes. Anyway I left this man none the wiser. But who needs an agent or PR with ex-girlfriends like that. All I can say to AAA is that the majority of *attempted* domestic murders are committed by people addicted to instant coffee. That is the evil we must fight.

A Bite of the Apple *12 April 1986*

Ten days in New York City was revitalizing and exhilarating although I spent far too much time in Bradley Cunningham's bar. Bradley's is, I think, the twin pub in America of Norman's Coach and Horses. Either that or P. J. Clarke's where there is some fairly serious organized loafing and kibitzing. But what a funny lot they are, these Americans. They actually take journalists seriously and have some respect for them whereas we know that journalists are simply shit-stirrers paid to drink on expenses. Ask Ian Botham. Anyway, it was rather odd to spend so much time with my boyhood hero Rocky Graziano, in and around Clarke's and with the oddball Jake La Motta. Both of them, made even more famous since their days in the ring by Paul Newman in *Somebody Up There Likes Me* and Robert de Niro in *Raging Bull*, still maintain their own peculiar identities.

Rocky is simply charming. He is the only folk hero I have ever met. Everybody, but everybody, stops him in the street to say hello and I have never seen a man more universally liked. He dragged himself up from the Lower East Side to become champion of the world, has made a million and still does the few television commercials which keep him in the public eye. Jake can't make commercials any more. He seems slightly sour about the fact that *Raging Bull* exposed him as having been something of a psychopathic wife-beater in and around the time he won the title from Marcel Cerdan. He protests that he never *really* beat up his wife. 'If I'd really hit her', he says, 'I'd have killed her.' It is slightly naïve. Although they are lifelong friends they should meet in the ring now. Even at 64 years of age they would fill the Yankee Stadium. They make the most awful facetious jokes about each other and I suspect that the banter probably disguises a pretty genuine mutual dislike. Rocky says, 'I told Jake that his new wife was cheating on him with his best friend so he went home and shot his dog.' Jake responds by saying, 'Rocky is so mean he is writing a travel book called "New York On Nothing A Day".' But Rocky for me is on a par with Fred Winter, Lester and Tony Hancock. He is tickled pink that I once had a failed short-spell career in the ring and he calls me 'champ'. The title seemed to puzzle several bartenders who heard him call me that, who then did double-takes at my skeletal frame and English accent.

The accent seemed to go down well with the ladies though. When I closed my eyes and thought about Claude Rains and Basil Rathbone and not England they curled up with their paws in the air like hypnotized pussy cats. One very nice lady took me up-state for a weekend in the country by the Hudson River. The scenery was stunning. My behaviour was awful. I was stunned by my old pal Smirnoff. Which reminds me. I don't much care for the way Americans are into health. There is far too much jogging and far too many raised eyebrows at the sight of you lighting a cigarette and knocking back a refreshing gargle. What an awful place to be broke in. It would be very difficult to get a handout in New York. We in London are pretty nice to tramps and winos and they on their part have a certain amount of style. Tom Baker told me the other day that he gave a tramp a fiver and the man had the cheek to hold it up to the light to see if it was genuine.

What was extraordinary in New York and up the Hudson at Cold Spring was the freak weather. It was 79 degrees every day and last Wednesday, sitting outside a restaurant and having lunch on the sidewalk, I asked a waiter to pull down the blind since the sun was burning my back. To come home back here was awful, but how on earth could you live abroad if you have friends like I've got? What a wonderful bunch they are. I never thought it would be possible to miss Norman and his steak pie, mashed potatoes served from an ice-cream scoop, and cabbage, and the bill thrown into your face. It never dawned on me that I might also miss his mother wiping the bar in front of me with a dirty cloth and at the same time giving me the weather forecast for Golders Green. And how good to get back to the adrenalin-filled English racing scene. A nice man called Dick Johnsen took me to the races at Aqueduct and you can forget American racing. Same track, same shape, same pace. Hell for leather and no tactics. It seemed to excite some Hispanic hysterics but it left me cold. The amenities are good though. You can get served. I told the bartender that he had put ginger ale in my vodka instead of soda and he flatly denied it saying that I couldn't tell the difference. I was compelled to attach my hands to his lapels, pull him half over the bar and inform him that I had been drinking for a sufficient number of years to know the difference. They can be awfully rude you know. So much nicer to be back in the Coach and Horses being sworn at by Norman Balon.

Getting a Buzz

3 May 1986

I was sitting on a bar stool the other afternoon minding my business and a drink and talking in a desultory fashion to Richard the barman about the quantum theory when I suddenly became aware of an amazing conversation that was going on just behind me. I looked round and saw, sitting around a table, two teenage girls interviewing a pretty young thing who is an actress apparently on the verge of having lift-off to the stars. It's no wonder that most show business people are completely bananas as you may have noticed particularly when they step up to collect awards. Later, it transpired that the interviewers were from a magazine called *Just 17* although they sounded as though they might have been from *Now We Are Eight*. Anyway, it's very heady stuff being interviewed and you obviously have to learn the language which is particular to interviews.

'What do you like most about acting?' 'Well, you know, basically it gives me a tremendous buzz. I like a challenge.' (Up till then I'd always thought of a challenge as being something like a blocked-up lavatory to a plumber.) 'Do you prefer being on the stage or doing films?' 'Well, basically films are bursts of concentration. You're working as such for three minutes a day. It gives me a buzz but the theatre is more of a challenge.' (This girl must have been a bee in a previous incarnation.) 'You say it gives you a buzz, but is there anything you don't like about acting?' 'Well, basically [if I hear one more basically I am going to scream] to look good all the time is tiring and quite painful [don't we bloody well know it my dear] and it's quite a strain when you think that there are more unemployed people in this business than there are in . . . [ship building?] well anyway, it's one hell of a challenge.' (If she likes challenges so much why not write to Marvin Hagler for an invitation?) 'Is there any one part you would particularly like to play?' (King Lear?) 'Well, basically, I'd like to play everything.' (Jesus Christ, another vodka please, Richard, I too need a buzz.) 'How do you get on with other people in the business?' 'Well, there are certain American actors you have to admire and allow them their griping, but basically I really like them. They give me a terrific buzz.' (You really ought to buy yourself an orange-and-black-striped jersey.) 'Do you prefer comedy or straight parts?' (You're in a comedy now, silly.) 'I don't really care as long as I'm working and have a challenge.'

At this point I moved along the bar out of earshot feeling quite numbed by the buzzing and the ringing of the bell for seconds out of the challenger's corner. And it's funny to think that I once wanted to be an actor. I always thought it was like Joan Littlewood once told me: 'messing about on the stage with some of your mates'. But I did feel an absolute rotter when they had to move because I was laughing so much. She should have stayed. If you're going to play comedy then laughter should be music to the ears. Anyway, I understand how that girl feels. I get a tremendous buzz out of being a hack. Usually when I get paid, if not then at opening time. It is also a tremendous challenge. Take today. I've got to write a column for the *Sporting Life* an hour and a half ago. And try talking to an editor on the telephone in a packed pub pretending that you're at home slogging your guts out in solitude. What's more, we never get to hear the applause if there is any but the abusive letters keep rolling in. I think I might cry in a minute and very nearly did when she said that about it being tiring and painful to look good all the time. I stole a look into the mirror behind the bar and wished I was Dorian Gray. But I tell you, being a film star is money for old rope. Every time I've seen a star they're always smiling. That surely signifies something apart from an overloaded bank account. Mind you, village idiots smile all the time. Maybe stars get punch drunk from flattery? Maybe from being interviewed. Come to think of it I was interviewed the other day by Ena Kendall from the *Observer* for that page called 'A Room of My Own'. After she'd gone, I realized with horror, and I mean horror, that I had been taking myself *seriously* for the 45 minutes she was with me. That is the end. No wonder actors and politicians are quite mad. You have heard of Ronald Reagan, haven't you?

Iron Rations

10 May 1986

She who would iron 14 shirts at one standing has been described by her daughter as being too compliant. I think this means obedient and it just isn't true. I haven't asked or expected of a woman that she should lift a finger for me since I was last in the position to provide for one and that was about 20 years ago. All I expect is that they wake me up when the waiter brings the bill. Shirt ironing is a voluntary occupation and it is very good therapy for a seething mind. It is also a pretty rare occurrence. Ever since 1960 or thereabouts, when the Beatles and feminism came to power and destroyed the civilization I was rather fond of, women have proved their independence by not only not ironing shirts but by not doing anything for half the human race. I think I might open an account with a proper laundry. I can't take any more recriminations from 17-year-olds for the sake of a stiff collar.

Otherwise it has been a pretty normal week. That's to say hardly any work has been done and yet I managed to get to Newmarket for the 2,000 Guineas. It was a very odd and very good day. I didn't set foot on the course but spent the afternoon in a friend's house eating and drinking and watching the wretched racing crowd on the television. What a bunch they are, the men with their strange hats and the women with their Hermès scarves. I wonder who does their ironing. But the strange thing was that I took an ex-wife with me, the one who is the mother of my daughter. This must have been the result of my having an extremely compassionate nature while she on her part likes lame dogs and probably should have been a vet. It's rather puzzling to me that I manage to stay friends with ex-wives and ex-girlfriends and I rather fear it may be because they consider me harmless like a defused bomb. Or maybe a snake with the venom removed.

Whenever I go to Newmarket I usually drop in to see another ex-wife who runs a club in Cambridge. I think she dreads race meetings at Newmarket because of my lurching into her bar after the last race. It probably brings back the most awful memories for her. When we were married we used to have an open house on Derby and Grand National days. I would cook a load of paella and a lot of friends including a bookmaker would come round and we had some jolly days. It's funny. I can't quite remember just what went wrong with that particular marriage. I vaguely think that she fell in love with my best friend which would have been par for the course. He was a handsome devil and now I choose my friends more carefully. They are a very nasty ugly bunch indeed. Think about it. Would your wife go off with Norman? Not on your nelly. She'd cling on to you for dear life if she saw that man approach. But then they say that there is someone for everyone. I don't believe it. On the other hand the Japanese didn't have any trouble in recruiting kamikaze pilots during the war. And I suppose if I advertised for a woman with a steam iron and ironing board that someone might just step into the firing line.

But, from now on, there are going to be fewer problems of that ilk in Soho. We now have a resident agony aunt. Irma Kurtz has moved to Soho and she will personally be lumbered with my wildest dreams, hopes, fears and shirts. I might even buy her an iron. Actually, there should be a mad competition to find the woman least likely to iron you a shirt. I would make Miriam Margolyes odds-on favourite, Vanessa Redgrave 5–4, Mrs Thatcher 2–1, Carmen Callil 7–2, Joanna Lumley 4–1, 100–8 bar. Although as we know ironing shirts is bourgeois revisionist I could be doing Ms Callil a disfavour. Like a lot of women I suspect she has a dreadful secret, i.e. she likes men. I have heard the same thing said about Edna O'Brien but that is mere hearsay from a waiter in the Gay Hussar. Meanwhile, I am down to my last six shirts. Help.

Flights of Fancy

17 May 1986

I was trying to drink a cup of tea in my bath this morning and I dropped it in the water. I didn't get out at once but lay there in the hot brown water in a sort of resigned despair. Have we travelled thus far, I thought, to end up resembling a tea bag? It wouldn't have happened to a winner. But then when I did get up and about and fetched the *Times*, there was good news. Cyd Charisse is here in England. She has brought her legs with her too, as you could have seen by the photograph of her on the back page. This woman has probably destroyed more of my brain cells than anything that ever came out of Russia, Finland or Warrington. I have given her a lot of thought, as have many other men of my age. When I was at school we used to be besotted with film stars. I remember writing a fan letter to Veronica Lake and to my surprise getting a signed photograph of her which I pinned to the underside of my desk lid. Rita Hayworth was poured into a silver lamé dress in *Gilda* and in *The Lady From Shanghai* she was breathtaking. We corresponded. Then there was Ava Gardner in *The Killers* and looking at her in that I felt as though I had been winded by a punch to the stomach.

But I have also fancied some really rather ropy actresses. This may be because one is caught up in a sartorial time warp. Virginia Mayo and Rhonda Fleming spring to mind and groin. Anne Sheridan, the Oomph Girl, was another. She started the business of sweaters. I am not what is commonly called a 'tit man' but there was something quite extraordinary about the aggressive thrust of her bust. But I am determined to meet Cyd Charisse. There are reservations though. My fantasies are destroyed by the idea of calling a beautiful woman Cyd or Sid and she happens to be married to that singer Tony Martin. Years ago when I was cavorting on the edge of an open-air swimming pool in Roehampton, he walked around the edge of it asking all the girls who were stretched out on the edge of it, 'Do you know who I am? I'm Tony Martin.' Yuck. The other thing I noticed apropos Cyd Charisse was that the *Guardian* very typically cropped her ankles and feet out of their picture of her. This was probably in deference to the dreadful people who read their ghastly woman's and education pages. Since Miss Charisse's legs go up to her throat perhaps they should have cropped her head.

So who is there now? Is it simply age or isn't there anybody about to be besotted with? My current obsessions are ordinary women who have not appeared on the silver screen. Even my cleaning lady looks sensational when she wields the Hoover. Which reminds me, apart from tea in the bath, I found an omelette on the floor yesterday morning. What happens at night is something of a mystery to me and I suppose the only way to find out just what does happen is to get hold of a television camera and to record everything from about 7 p.m. onwards. I am still trying to solve the mystery of the curry I found in one of my shoes. Another mystery was the note I found recently on the bedside table which just said, 'Would you like to try again some time?' It wasn't even signed. As I have previously reported, I have woken up in King's Lynn and at Bristol Temple Mead on the last train, but an omelette on the carpet is quite disconcerting. On close inspection I noticed that I or a mystery person had made it a cheese omelette, which denotes a certain amount of care and ambition. I was disappointed though on looking under the bed not to find a side salad.

The other thing I found recently on waking was an invitation to the annual dinner at the Royal Academy. It is almost unbelievable. Why me? Can they be simply asking people who know what they like this year? I have brothers who ooze poetry and art but I am a humble omelette-dropper who thinks that Giacometti was third in the Derby carrying Charles St George's colours. It means a dinner jacket of course, this dinner, and I hope I don't find anything strange in it the following morning. I still haven't recovered from the shock of finding an uncooked, shish kebab in my blazer pocket last week.

Smiling all the Way *7 June 1986*

Ah, sweet mystery of life. Well, not sweet really and pretty trivial but nonetheless quite perplexing. A couple of days ago, when I woke up and got out of bed, I found a paper-clip in my pubic hair. I don't keep paper clips and I am not having an affair with a secretary. As I say, a mystery. I could have understood a morsel of, say, Chinese takeaway, but a paper-clip is odd to say the least. It was what Holmes would have called a five pipe problem. Anyway I searched for rubber bands and drawing pins but found no accomplices and took myself off to the Clermont Club for lunch with a friend who is a sort of cockney Taki and who can afford such treats. What an extraordinary place the Clermont is. It is certainly extremely ornate being as it is seemingly constructed out of gold leaf but isn't it really rather vulgar? I had a look upstairs in the gaming room although play hadn't commenced and I saw one table with a notice which said that the minimum stake for punters was £100 and the maximum stake £10,000. You'd think people would have better things to do with their money, but no. What really staggered me was to learn on the internal grapevine that there is one Arab who is permitted £1 million's worth of credit a day. Yes, a day. Mind you, I'm quite glad not to have been born an Arab. I could have woken up with a camel in my bed instead of a harmless paper-clip. And anyway such gamblers can never feel the pleasure of fear. To put oneself at risk and then to get out can be very stimulating. The lunch in the club was quite interesting. I kicked off with a mixture of avocado, crabmeat and cheese – cooked – and then grilled for a minute or two. Then I had roast duck served with a blackcurrant sauce. Very good. Then I broke the hospital rules and finished with some chocolate cake with cream. But what I kept thinking about during that lunch, apart from paper-clips, was what an awful job to be a waiter or restaurant manager. I mean, can you imagine having to be nice to every stranger and also smile at them? It's hard enough to smile at somebody you're married to. And they like to go over the top a bit too. A man insisted on his carrying my drink on a tray from the bar to the restaurant, a distance of 10 yards. Smiling all the way, of course. They like to baby you but this baby doesn't want his rattle taken away from him for even a ten yard sprint. Gaston Berlemont in the French pub had the best waiter I've ever known. Unbeknown to Gaston he used to spoof me for the bill. He was a lousy spoof player and eventually I got so confident I'd go upstairs to eat when I was skint and I mean skint. That was a nice little risk in those bygone days although adrenalin doesn't sit easily on boeuf bourguignon and Moulin au Vent. He must have been almost 70 that waiter and the poor old chap had Parkinson's. Everyone mistook the shaking for a massive hangover. He won £5,000 on the pools one day, had a few drinks and gave a lot of it away. The wine waiter had brown snuff stains around his nostrils which wasn't so pretty. But what a good restaurant that was. But, as I say, what a dreadful job. Can you imagine serving prawn cocktails and then Chicken Maryland to a lot of twits at a Rotary lunch in a Rotary lunch-orientated dump like Chelmsford? I think the Rotarians may possibly be an offshoot of the National Front. I certainly don't like waitresses in restaurants. Barmaids I like but not waitresses. I haven't been to it for years but Sheekey's had waitresses, mostly middle-aged and nice but they all smelled of talcum powder or lavender and there was considerable fallout into the sole. Next to Sheekey's at the Round Table pub there was a guvnor who thought he could fly when he was drunk. He found great difficulty in taking off in the saloon so he would go upstairs and jump out of the window into Cecil Court. He was very resilient. Come to think of it there is a first class waitress and that is Mary in the Coach and Horses. Which brings me to that avaricious hard nut, Norman. The other day he lifted up his dear old mum's hand which carries about £50,000 worth of diamonds on it and started an oration on how he thought voluntary euthanasia is a good thing. Some people have no shame. But who has the paper-clips?

Taking a Break

5 July 1986

The media – what a loathsome word – has spent one hell of a lot of time and space on Richard Branson this past week enthusing about his Atlantic power boat crossing and I'm up to here with it. How quickly a man may cross the Atlantic is as irrelevant to me as is how quickly a man may walk from Holland Park to Lancaster Gate. And thank the Lord that the World Cup is over. Once Wimbledon is finished there will, with luck, be no news at all. I don't mind if Fleet Street and television take a long break although I would like to keep in touch with England's cricketing humiliations for the next two months. Yes, I'm so fed up with news I think I'll switch to the awful *Sun* which contains nothing. The trouble is I am addicted to the *Times*. It is a fix of sorts. I hasten to add that I am not being paid by them to say so, in fact I don't seem to be getting paid by anyone at the moment. It is only fair to warn all you seething undergraduates wishing to become hacks that the bastards keep you waiting for three months sometimes while they accrue interest on your money. It is also a fact that all accountants can't bear to part with money since they unconsciously regard it as theirs. There must be some other way to earn a living that doesn't involve keeping office hours. I had hoped to be left in charge of the Coach and Horses while Norman was on holiday in Sicily, but no. He must be suffering. He hates the sea, beaches, the sun, sand and lying about doing nothing. He even took three friends with him on his honeymoon years ago so that he could while away the time playing cards. There's romance for you. She was probably quite relieved. (The thought of being swept into his arms has made me reach for the bottle and it's only 9.30 a.m.) You could see for yourself if this column was illustrated.

But speaking of holidays I am going away to Portugal for a few days. I have never been there but I gather there is nothing to eat save grilled sardines. I am also told that there are no less than eight golf courses where I am going so there should be hundreds of really horrendous Englishmen. I have friends who play golf but I like them one at a time. But what worries me most about Portugal is returning to the boat at night and negotiating the gangplank. To be eaten by sardines and subsequently English golfers is not the end I have in mind. Anyway, there's no escaping Fleet Street because Barclays Bank is so voracious. I phoned a column over from a Greek island once in a beach bar while a local girl rubbed sun oil into my back and that wasn't too unpleasant but it's tricky in Barbados after a few rum punches and mild sunstroke. The only thing that cheers me up about phoning Fleet Street from abroad is that whenever I have said to the copy-taker, 'What's the weather like in London?' they have always replied, 'It's pissing down.' So comforting. But I don't know why I'm having this little holiday at all really. Wherever I go I am there. People are always saying, 'it'll do you good to get away.' Why will it? Don't they realize it is myself I want to get away from or are they in truth saying it will do *them* good? At least Norman misses me when I go away. 'What you want to go and spend your money somewhere else for?' he screams. Fancy phoning from Sicily to have the manager read out the till roll.

But to get back to the bad news. I have just been told over the telephone – what a horrid blunt instrument – that Branson's winning journey has 'lifted the hearts of Britons after our defeat in the World Cup'. Perhaps Mrs Thatcher will consider it a fitting moment for a general election.

Travellers' Tales

26 July 1986

Well, I wasn't drowned in Portugal after all. I came home last week, though, to find I have been served with a bankruptcy order. You win some, you lose some. Anyway, the weather was splendid and the grilled sardines, chips and salads kept me in surprisingly good nick. The only trouble was that the boat's bilge pump was out of action. This meant we had to run ashore at the crack of dawn every day to use the lavatory in the nearest café. Once there it was lovely to have a glass of freshly squeezed orange juice, but you can't drink that all morning so at about 8 a.m. I had to switch to lager, not that I like it much. At 10 a.m. I reckoned it was a sort of opening time and so went back to the orange with some vodka in it. Now, dear reader, I must warn you of the perils of falling asleep in the sun. Don't. Prickly heat is ghastly and I had such an awful headache I had to hold a chilled bottle of white wine to my fevered brow. It was very soothing in much the same way as a cold lavatory pan is when pressed against the forehead when one is being sick. (This happens frequently after opening buff envelopes.)

But talking of being sick, what about Scandinavian tourists? They must be the most boring travelling circus in the world. Can it be because of their long nights? Tom Baker thinks the rot set in when English critics pronounced that *Hedda Gabler* was boring when it was first produced. Perhaps they feel *obliged* to be boring. You hear men verbally drooling about Scandinavian au pair girls but in reality those blue eyes are vacuous and even the blondeness is boring. Their hair looks like cornflakes. I once had a few hours at Stockholm airport and a single gin and tonic cost £3.50. Perhaps that is why they look dumbstruck and it probably explains the high suicide rate.

But the English in and around Faro were fascinating. I suppose it is because the Portuguese are our oldest allies that we import their port and they import our bank robbers. There must be some sort of trade agreement between the two of us. I got the impression that it is obligatory to have knocked over an English bank in order to get a resident's permit there. There was a delightful con man there too who was a mine of information on the subject of the English penal system. But most amazing of all was an alcoholic woman who claimed to be a psychotherapist. She was legless from Marble Arch to Christmas. Now although I realize that social workers feel obliged from time to time to murder the children in their charge I do think it is reasonable to expect a little sobriety from a brain manipulator. I mean *somebody's* got to be sober. I must say, talking of psychotherapy, how much I enjoyed the tiny spell of it I had when I was banged up in the addiction slammer. One day an awful fellow patient enraged me so much that I leapt upon him and tried to strangle him. It took half the ward to pull me off him. It was quite delightful. Forty years of anger out of the system in a few seconds. I'd quite like to meet that man again because there's some subsequent anger been building up. Anyway, this woman had a delightful little girl – her husband had left her – and I kept wondering what will become of her. With luck she might react and grow up to be something of a Puritan. I sometimes wish that my parents had been a little more wayward. Had they been so I now might be a magistrate or a milkman. The sentences heavy and the milk sour. But funny things holidays, aren't they? I can't wait for them and yet I am always pleased to get back to this rat hole which I feel so safe in despite being surrounded by danger. Danger of duns. They'll be coming through the windows next. I actually had a man in the sitting-room this morning who made me write out eight post-dated cheques. I tried to imagine I was writing out betting slips or signing traveller's cheques but the hand was shaking too much to fool the imagination. But before the final crunch comes I shall, like Custer, have one last stand at Ascot on Saturday to see the King George VI and Queen Elizabeth Diamond Stakes. It will be overcrowded, expensive and sweaty with anxiety when Shahrastani comes into the straight but it will be some sort of punctuation mark in the financial story. It's like turning over an old leaf.

Dog Days

2 August 1986

When I bet a friend of mine £200 last Saturday that Dancing Brave would finish in front of Shahrastani wherever they finished I didn't feel particularly nervous until we sat down to have our picnic at Ascot. Then the butterflies began to fly. It wasn't the vichyssoise we were sipping – very good stuff for imbibers – it was the thought of wouldn't it be better to change and settle down. Later on in the afternoon when Dancing Brave hit the furlong pole I thought no it wouldn't be a good idea to change and settle down. This quandary strikes me with some force every morning when I open my eyes. God willing. I think it may be best to change and settle down for just a couple of hours every day until opening time. Anyway, I was a little irritated the next day to see the *Observer* describe me as being the *Spectator*'s Bohemian scribbler. I am about as Bohemian as Jack Dempsey and I have an electric typewriter not a pencil. So many people confuse Bohemian with drunken layabout or bum or would-be painter. There aren't any Bohemians left in Soho now, only a load of mostly clapped-out hacks. The last Bohemian I saw in Soho was Augustus John and that's going back a bit. But the word scribbler is derogatory which hack funnily enough isn't. It matters not a lot but then on Tuesday the *Racing Post* described me as being lovable and irrepressible. I might be lovable to a guide dog and I'm very repressible. What a strange thing to say. Then he went on to call me the somewhat inebriated *Spectator* columnist. I'm not sure about the somewhat. Either you're pissed or you're not.

But I met a bookmaker friend at Ascot who told me a very hard luck story. He has a greyhound dog which was quite good on the track and which he recently retired to stud. It should have brought him in about £300 a week in stud fees. The bookmaker also bought two bitches for £1,500 so that he could help himself to a couple of litters. Now what's choked him is that it turns out that the dog just can't do the business. All it does apparently is eat like a horse. I suggested it might be because the dog had an unhappy puppyhood or that someone in the kennels was feeding it vodka but it remains a mystery. Now he says he's going to try dressing the bitches up in frilly knickers and suspender belts.

Funny things dogs though. I don't have very good memories of the days when I used to go to the dogs literally. I used to go to New Cross on Saturday nights long ago to back the last favourite. One night I fell from near the top of the grandstand right down to the bottom where the bookmakers stood. I must have negotiated nearly a hundred steps during that seemingly endless tumble. Then when I started in this awful business I had to go to Wembley to interview a bitch who had run up a tremendous sequence of wins. I don't know what you say to a dog but I couldn't even get a bark out of her. No, you can keep the dogs although I suppose it can be quite pleasant to have dinner at Wimbledon dogs of a summer's evening. You can imagine the food. It's what these people think is up-market when they go out. Chicken Maryland or gammon steaks. Both are very ordinary but they have both been awarded a ring of pineapple. Very classy.

Mind you, the catering at most proper racecourses isn't up to much although they do a passable curry at Sandown Park, so it will be picnics in future and flasks of soup during the National Hunt time of year. I suppose one could save a fortune by taking one's own booze. I took a bottle of Pernod to Newbury races some years ago when I was addicted to pastis and it affected my judgment badly. My binoculars didn't seem to like it much either. Which reminds me. I brought back a bottle of absinthe from Portugal out of sheer curiosity. We opened it the other day and it is awful. With water it goes not yellow, it is green. But I could tell after a couple that the French government were quite sensible to ban it. Gaston Berlemont says it was banned because it made men impotent and women infertile. I suspect it was because it made the working classes go blind.

Weighed Down

16 August 1986

I spent three hours in the Middlesex clinic a couple of days ago and they said they weren't happy about my legs. Neither am I. But at least they said I could keep them for a while longer. My brother says I don't walk enough but where is there to walk to? Lands End? Certainly walking in London is no longer a pleasure now that everyone uses the streets as rubbish dumps. I still keep trying to picture in my mind just how the hell you get in and out of a taxi with one leg. In the event of what my parrot calls a double Long John Silver I suppose the thing would be to hire an au pair girl and stay in bed for good. But none of this nonsense matters. What does worry me is what on earth must the man be like who disposes of these human parts in the hospital incinerator? And don't tell me 'somebody has got to do it'. Nobody has to do anything except breathe. When I spent a day in the theatre in 1969 watching operations (I was writing about a surgeon), I saw some very strange things go into the pedal bin.

But no, it's not the legs it's the weight. They weigh you every time you go to the clinic and I think I am wasting so much that I shall eventually disappear up my own arse. Someone told me a strange story the other day about an Australian woman who was a compulsive eater. She lived in a clapboard-type bungalow and stayed in it for 15 years eating sweets which she had delivered to her. She eventually became so fat and big that when she died they had to demolish the house to get her out. I shall be taken out of this flat in a matchbox and through the letterbox. Anyway, when I got home from the clinic I had to telephone British Telecom and there was no bloody answer. That could only happen in England, couldn't it? I tell you we are going down the drain.

I am not a sociologist, merely a spectator, but you would have to be blind not to see that people don't even eat properly any more. There must be a colossal chemical imbalance in this country beginning at 10 Downing Street and ending up in Coronation Street. Years ago, when I was deeply depressed and had no idea of the necessary survival kit required for this three score and ten years' amble, a Harley Street man looked me over and said it was purely a matter of chemistry. It was then that I switched from whisky to vodka. Perhaps Marie Antoinette's advice to her people was sound medical stuff although my brother claims she was badly translated and in fact advised them to eat brioche. What I wonder do Manchester United supporters eat. Perhaps the decline of our society began with the chip. I gather that Vikings used to eat toadstools to help them go berserk so I think it possible that football hooligans behave as they do because of a surfeit of chips and steamed pud with custard. I don't know what they eat at Downing Street but I did have tea there once. Lord Wigg gave me a perfectly dreadful cup of tea and a rock cake *à la* British Rail. What a self-righteous man he was.

Anyway, I eat pretty well but I'm damned if I can put on an ounce. In 1950 when I was boxing I wanted to put on three pounds and my trainer made me put a teaspoonful of powdered gelatine into my cup every time I took tea. It was fairly revolting and might possibly explain the final hammering I took. But nowadays it is almost impossible to eat out – and I am out and about – unless you have an expense account. Hence the crazy prices in restaurants. In an effort to economize I have used the Chinese places in Gerrard Street quite a lot and have duck and rice coming out of my ears. But that doesn't put on weight and rice could be as dangerous as chips, as you might know if you have ever seen a Chinaman lose his temper. It's frightening. Anyway, I can't remember ever having seen a fat Chinaman except for Charlie Chan. The calorie problem for those whose pancreas is up the creek is a stalemate. I resign. I shall now have just the one and forget all about it. Everything.

Thrill-a-Minute

6 September 1986

Yet another idiot student approached me yesterday and among other things said how exciting it must be to be a hack. Well, of course it is. Take this morning. I woke up with an excruciating pain in my back to discover I'd been sleeping on a Langan's

Brasserie cocktail stick all night, then discovered that the milk had gone off and then opened the post to discover a royalty cheque from *Punch* for £5. I then found a note from the cleaning lady which said, 'We need Flash, bathroom cleaner, Harpic and furniture polish.' Now I'm pretty sure that a man like D'Artagnan didn't start his day like that and I am certain that the life Reilly led in no way resembled that, but this young man would have it that I am somewhere half-way between the two of them. If he only knew it, that note from the cleaning lady is the nearest I've been to a love letter in five years. What these people don't realize is that it is they who are to be envied what with their punting beautiful girls up the river and getting grants to read books. (What they substitute for punting in red-brick universities I wonder about.)

But the young man would be saved a lot of aggravation if only he could be the fly on my wall and behold the cobwebs on my typewriter. Even my house plants have got lung cancer. The skin of an old melon has been lying on my desk for three days and I'm too depressed to move it. It awaits the return of the cleaning lady. I never see her. She has her own set of keys and descends on these shambles every Wednesday and I wonder just what the hell she makes of it. Sherlock Holmes would see at a glance that he was in the flat of a man who has surrendered. The young student though would probably think the overflowing ashtrays, dirty glasses and dirty-tissue-filled wastepaper basket to be fearfully exciting.

The builder Mike Molloy told me about got it right though. This man was laying tiles on the kitchen floor of a woman colleague's house. There he was on his hands and knees and half covered in cement when he asked our friend, 'What do you do for a living?' She said, 'I'm a newspaper columnist.' He looked up at her and said, 'God, how boring.' What an incredibly happy and foolish man he must be.

And how foolish of the student to come out with that silly old chestnut of how exciting it must be for us to be able to meet *famous* people. Oh yeah? I was with a famous person the other day without realizing it. She who would have me barred from the Groucho Club for my bad language turns out to be none other than Dale Spender the Australian militant feminist and, I quote from a book blurb, 'a writer from choice and necessity, a feminist who has set herself the task of drawing attention to the sexist nature of our language' de dah, de dah, and so on. Well, the club lent me two of her books and so full of hate are they that it burnt my fingers to turn the pages. The antipodean feminist must be the most fearsome and tortured animal on earth. I shall return the books to the club today as gingerly as if I were disposing of nuclear waste. Far from exploiting women I don't even notice them any more. So sucks, boo, yah, if you'll forgive the language. Yesterday, when I went into the club I felt so nervous of seeing Ms Spender that it was as though I'd had a large dose of amphetamine. Oh yes, young man, my life as a hack is full of excitement. I mean once you've had tea with Raquel Welch and Princess Margaret, a cocktail with Anthony Burgess and a row with Norman Mailer what else is there left? Not a lot. Later, after I go out to plunder the supermarkets of Flash, bathroom cleaner, Harpic and furniture polish I shall go to the pub for some exciting conversation and, of course, a pain-killing drink. Gordon will tell me how he failed by a short head yesterday to win a fortune. The barman will tell me of a football result that I have not the slightest interest in hearing about. Norman will tell me that he is about to get a cold and that the telephone is out of order. His mother will tell me that it rained in Hendon last night. Any one of half a dozen women will give me a reproachful look for nothing I can remember doing or not doing. Graham will ask me, 'What did I do last night?' Terrific stuff. Really exciting, isn't it?

Pot-boiler

13 September 1986

A detective I know fixed it for me to have a guided tour of the Black Museum in New Scotland Yard this week after I had casually mentioned to him that I am morbidly fascinated by murder. I think most people probably are and I must say it was quite riveting to find myself face to face with Nilsen's kitchen stove with the catering-size boiling pan on top of it. The stove hasn't been cleaned and there are transfers of butterflies on the oven door. Next to it there is Nilsen's bath. A murderer can't afford to be squeamish I thought. And looking at photographs of Jack the Ripper's victims I thought how lucky that I'm not particularly squeamish either. No doctor could have committed those murders, as some have speculated.

But to kick off with, the man in charge of the museum, a criminologist and forensic expert of renown, showed us the weapons that are available to almost everybody in cities today. Apart from an arsenal of small arms, all lethal and extremely nasty, there was one curio that was food for thought. It was a golf ball spiked with nails on the end of a chain with a handle to hold it by while wielding it. It was made by an eight-year-old boy who told the police that he got the idea from his parents' video nasties. When the law called round and asked the parents did they know their boy watched these videos they said yes they did, they wanted him to expand his horizons and would the police mind their own business. The boy had just nearly blinded one of his school chums and I suppose you've got to start somewhere.

Probably the most gruesome exhibit and a marvellous example of German efficiency is a man's two arms in a glass tank of formaldehyde. They belonged to a man wanted for questioning by the Yard about his wife's murder. They heard that a man had shot himself dead in Germany and they asked the police there to send them his fingerprints to see if he was the same one they were after. But the Germans are nothing if not thorough. So they sent the arms and hands. Who needs photocopies? I stared at this tank of limbs exactly like something from a Frankenstein movie and thought what the hell am I doing here? Yesterday I was at Longchamp drinking champagne all day and being hosted by the senior stewards of the French Jockey Club in autumnal sunshine and here I am the next day looking at bits and pieces of somebody.

Next to the arms there was evidence of Haigh's blunders. You can't blame him for not having known that concentrated sulphuric acid can't dissolve gall stones but you can see a pair of dentures when they're staring you in the face. But what a strange man he must have been to have made the dying request that Madame Tussaud's should have his *real* clothes after his hanging. I lived just around the corner from him when he was dissolving rich women and I once lived in a terrible dump around the corner from Rillington Place. I sometimes wonder if I ever passed the time of day with Christie in a cafe or pub. And how odd that the two most horrendous murderers of this century, Christie and Nilsen, should both at one time have been policemen. But even the trivia – visual trivia – in the Black Museum have a strange appeal: soup tins on which the Great Train Robbers left the fingerprints that got them caught, and the gun Ruth Ellis used, plus the minute pellet from the umbrella which killed the Bulgarian.

After the tour the detectives took me for a drink, well needed especially because of champagne dehydration. The things these people have to look at. The worst, I ventured in my imagination, would be to find somebody who had been dead for a while in their flat during a hot summer. 'I'd feel distinctly edgy', I said, 'to see a row of milk bottles growing every day.' 'Oh, you don't need to worry about the milk bottles outside,' said my CID man, 'it's the bluebottles inside.' Since that day I keep seeing Nilsen's gas stove in my mind's eye and I have just been into the kitchen to look at mine and it looks so harmless sitting there patiently waiting to boil an egg. Nilsen's somehow didn't and it might have been those transfers of butterflies stuck on it. At the Yard it is rumoured that he is cracking now and will end up in Broadmoor. I wonder he didn't go there straight from the dock.

Pleas and Peas

27 September 1986

There is something rather disconcerting about appearing before an attractive woman magistrate although, heaven knows, there shouldn't be for a man like me who has been married four times. In those days I suppose you could say that I was up before the beak every morning. My applications for bail to go to the races or go to the pub were usually granted but there was always a frost in the air. No wonder they use the word 'plea' in the world of litigation. But obviously I can't talk to you about my forthcoming trial on 20 October save to say that while I am on remand the Customs & Excise people will be making, in the words of the prosecutor, 'extensive inquiries'. My oldest friends are already fleeing this sinking ship. One of them telephoned me today to say that it would be bad to be seen with me from now on and warned me that I could expect the Customs men to come and break my front door in. And what would they find? An unmade bed and a wreck of a man who in Fran Landesman's immortal words is 'drinking his lunches/losing his nerve'. The other thing that saddens me in this third-rate Indian summer is that the *Daily Mail* can't spell my name correctly. Neither could the court usher pronounce it properly.

Otherwise, apart from being arrested, interrogated and fingerprinted, it has been a perfectly splendid week punctuated by afternoon teas in the Groucho Club, cocktails there and at the scene of the alleged crime and dalliance in bed with *Middlemarch*. It is in that book, as my friend who now wishes to avoid me pointed out, that George Eliot perfectly describes a member of the SDP. Of Mr Brooke she writes, 'a man of acquiescent temper, miscellaneous opinions and uncertain vote'. But then, casting *Middlemarch* aside on Wednesday morning, I leapt from bed and into the pinstriped suit and went to Boodle's for luncheon with two barristers. I wouldn't exactly call that a slice of low life although there is a betting book there as there is in White's. I seem to remember one odd bet which the Duke of Wellington struck with a chum. He bet him £50 that his footman could run 100 yards faster than the other man's footman. But nowadays, that might contravene section 2(1) of the Betting, Gaming and Lotteries Act, 1963; unless, of course, he was a member of Boodle's or White's or that wretched haven of suburban spivs, the Turf Club. I have lived in hope for some time now that Taki would make me a member of Annabel's but he too is avoiding me. A pity really since I long to know how it feels to pay £5 for an ordinary drink. I wonder, does it hurt? Probably, but the paradox is that half a dozen of them would nullify the agony. You can imagine how recent events have driven me to drink in spite of the fact that my local rip-off merchant charges 35p for each lousy orange that my vodka craves. Some mornings I can hear it crying in the fridge. It stops when I take it out and then gurgles like a contented baby. She who would iron 14 shirts at one standing bought me an electric juice squeezer and I love it so much I think I might die of vitamin C poisoning.

Incidentally I think the whole thing about vitamins is a bit nonsensical. If you eat the right stuff you shouldn't need supplementary vitamins. I have recently become addicted to the liver pâté and chutney sandwiches that the dairy in Frith Street sells. I can't eat Norman's stuff any more since he has switched to horribly healthy, good bread. It has grains of wheat in it the size of brazil nuts and my teeth just aren't up to it. Even he sneaks out to buy his sandwiches from M&S. And talking of food, you know I have found strange things in this room like curry in my bedroom slippers, well, this morning I found some frozen peas in the bedside ashtray. I think there is a night-time gnome in this flat who has escaped from a Beatrix Potter book and I wish he'd go away and drive somebody else potty. I take full responsibility for the sweet-corn in the video machine but I draw the line at peaing in an ashtray. Perhaps I am going mad. I hope not. That would contravene section 2(1) of the Keep Right On Till The End Of The Road Act, 1986. I don't think I can take any more trouble. Oh God. And now the vodka has started crying again. I shall have to go and see to it.

Up Hill, Down Dale

4 October 1986

It is difficult to concentrate with the sword of Damocles – once sheathed in West End Central police station – hanging over me, but I am aware of the fact that I have a cold, cough, sore throat and headache and that it is a grey day outside. In spite of that I can't help wondering whether watching the Arc de Triomphe on Sunday at Longchamp while on bail will constitute high life or low life. I am being hounded by horses. If New Scotland Yard had any sense of theatre they would have had me arrested by mounted policemen. Yes, one minute it's Paris and the next minute it's the courtroom and something happens almost every day to remind me of that good old Arab proverb, 'Life is like a banana. One minute it is in your hand and the next minute it is up your arse.' This morning I dropped a soft-boiled egg on the floor but tonight Taki is taking me out on the town, an exercise I shall have to train for by sleeping all afternoon. The stamina's gone, you see. And then, between that and Paris there is the party in Brighton to celebrate 25 years of *Private Eye* and the retirement of Richard Ingrams. So it's all go. The constant demands that are made on my metabolism, pocket, solicitor and liver are very exhausting.

But the really bad news this week concerns not the CID, horses or the results of liver function tests but the dreaded Dale Spender, the woman who would have me barred for my language. I was told the other day, on good authority, that she once actually told her female students that they 'should be rude to a man or men three times a day'. It staggers me. In fact I have not been so staggered since I last wore 8oz gloves. I hadn't realized that we had actually had war declared on us. I thought there was just a bit of banter in the wind. But no, we shall have to take up arms. No longer will I drape my extremely expensive Crombie overcoat over puddles for women to step on and no longer will I allow them to drown in my eyes. If they want to play rough we'll see who can be ruder. And all the time I thought they were friends. I must have been running in blinkers. The next time a woman smiles at me – and one did yesterday – I shall not let it go to my head but merely remind myself that we once played football with the Germans in no-man's land on Christmas Day.

And now here's a funny thing. Just two minutes ago the postman brought me a letter from Ohio written by a man who reads this journal and who works in a liquor store in a town called Hiram. He says that if I am ever in the Cleveland area he will give me the pick of the litter from the store on condition I go to an AA meeting with him. Having been once forced to attend AA meetings when I was in the bin 15 years ago I can tell you, Mr Killey – for that is he – that wild horses couldn't drag me to one of those evangelical, smug, told-you-so, wasn't-I-awful gatherings again. And the AA handout is perfectly dreadful that you sent me. Alcohol has not got me 'licked'. Women had me 'licked' once but not since I met Dale Spender. She constitutes a meeting of Womanizers Anonymous all by herself. Try substituting the word 'women' for the word 'drinking' in the AA questionnaire. Are women affecting your peace of mind? Are women making your home life unhappy? Do you show marked moodiness since women? Are women disturbing the harmony of your life? Have women changed your personality? Do you crave a woman at a definite time daily? Do you require a woman the next morning? Do you prefer a woman alone? Have women made you irritable? Yes, yes, yes, and again yes. And as for asking me have I ever felt remorse after drinking, Mr Killey, I have been living with remorse for years now. She wakes me up every morning. She puts me to bed at night and yea though I run through the valley of Oxford Street to the Coach and Horses she is by my side. Now why don't you and the girl you don't want to wake up by using a typewriter (yes, you do scrawl) come over here for a holiday and we can rescue you from your wagon. We put our wagons in a circle once but the Indians still won. Thank God.

Win Some, Lose Some

11 October 1986

Last Sunday's Prix de l'Arc de Triomphe in Paris was something to write home about and I would have done so if there had been anybody at home. Dancing Brave is half a ton of bone and muscle sheathed in bay velvet, a matchless machine of an animal. He glistens like something well oiled and polished. I managed to get into the pre-parade ring by the stables to have a look at them all before the race and he was walking around looking cool and lazy in the way Sugar Ray Robinson did just a second before he knocked you out. Now they are saying he is one of the greatest horses since the war. Make that one of the greatest since the thoroughbred was invented.

The pleasure and luck of having been there to witness the race was hardly diminished by the fact that some French yob stole my luggage at Boulogne on the way home. Dancing Brave is worth more than four shirts, four pants, four pairs of socks, a blazer, a pair of jeans, a toothbrush and a roll of exposed film taken in the Père Lachaise that I was going to sell to a glossy magazine alongside some deathless guff about the majority of Frenchmen only pleasing me when six feet under in the Père Lachaise. Who the hell cut off the balls of the figure on the ghastly Epstein-designed tomb of Oscar Wilde is anybody's guess. My guess is that it was an antipodean feminist. Anyway, some old crone still puts violets on Chopin's grave every day which is right and proper.

The day before the race a friend took me on a walk around the Bastille area and showed me the church of St Gervais where Couperin played and the house Mozart dazzlingly tinkled in as a young boy. Before that, at 8 a.m., I was sipping a beer as insomniacs are wont to, in a cafe where there was a punch-up. My French stinks but I gathered that the two men involved, accompanied by two prostitutes, had been discussing sex, which is not in my opinion a subject for conversation before 11 a.m., official British opening time in most parts. Cyrano de Bergerac died just around the corner from that place and you wouldn't be surprised. I was so close to the two contestants it was a miracle that I didn't get a glass stuck in the haggard face.

But apart from English horses it is Englishmen who make this first weekend in October for me one of the best of the year. The hospitality of bookmaker Victor Chandler and of Rocco Forte who sponsors the Arc is pretty fantastic. We had a splendid lunch at Victor's hotel before the racing started on Sunday and then I watched the big race itself from the balcony outside Rocco Forte's suite in the grandstand. I watched the Dancing Brave acceleration sitting at a table with Peregrine Worsthorne and his wife, the only French charmer at Longchamp. Perhaps that's fractionally unfair to the French but you can certainly feel that they don't like us a lot. Max Hastings was there as well and for all I know Geoffrey Wheatcroft was probably under the table. It was an Indian summer of a day and an hour sitting at a table outside the paddock champagne bar watching the world go by was a delight. Those très chic French women must spend a fortune on their clothes and I can't help wondering where and how they get the loot for them. I think we should be told. Anyway, their husbands certainly should be told.

Just for once, coming home was awful. After the lost luggage at Boulogne I fell asleep on the train between Dover and Victoria and some bastard nicked my duty-free litre of real vodka plus 200 cigarettes. All these things will have to be replaced somehow and rich women don't fancy me any more. Then I had to spend an age with a solicitor who took down my statement about the impending court case on Monday week. And now I have just received a message to say that the Customs & Excise people are coming this morning to serve me with a summons. Sometimes I feel like a bone – and look like one – surrounded by dogs. Michael Heath once gave me the present of a cartoon in which a man standing at a bar is saying, 'I try to drown my troubles but they've learnt to swim.' Quite so. But at least I saw the greatest race and I shall be thinking of Dancing Brave and Victor's and Rocco's parties when I step up to the trap door. They're cruel, you know. They hang you before opening time.

Unsavoury Customs

25 October 1986

I still don't see why friends shouldn't be allowed to bet among themselves without interference from the Government, but never mind. The sentence of the court was a £200 fine, £75 costs and £31.12 in betting duty. I was told before going into the court that I could ask to be tried by jury in a crown court but that the case wouldn't come up for another 15 months. The only advantage I could see in putting it off for that length of time in the hope of finding a sympathetic jury was the consideration that I might have avoided the entire confrontation by dying within that time. That is always on the cards but knowing my bad luck I shall probably be betting on the Derby in 1996, a shadow of my former shadow. My lawyer made a really excellent speech to the magistrate but my friends in the gallery who came to lend me support, and in some cases write about it all, laughed too much and the beak didn't like the levity. To cap it all, at the time of writing, the wretched Customs & Excise people are still sitting on the ready money I had on me when I was arrested. They want to confiscate my £58. This is not over-zealousness but vindictive. I now have to prove to the bastards – and I can – that I cashed a cheque for £50 with Norman minutes before I was nicked. Not all the animals in London are confined to Regent's Park. My sainted lawyer told me that he thought the Customs & Excise men were 'dullards' and I wonder just what it is that makes young men choose such a career. They're still digging up the skeletons of their forerunners in Cornwall and Romney Marsh and they'll probably be digging them up in the Tottenham Court Road in a hundred years from now. Am I in a replay of *Les Miserables*?

Mind you I am grateful to them for having driven me to drink. I hadn't realized that up to the time I was arrested I had merely been toying with the stuff.

But isn't it odd that the people who make the law are above it. There is quite a lot of serious punting in the House of Commons and that I *do* know. I also know who makes the book and he was a Cabinet minister at one time. Anyway, I am going to get rid of the bad smell, so to speak, and I'm off on a freebie to Tunisia today. To be more precise I am going to an island off the coast of Tunisia called Kerkenna. I suppose that inevitably there will be a large man of Sidney Greenstreet proportions sitting behind a newspaper by a palm in the hotel lobby. The good news though is that I am going alone. Never again will I travel in a group of hacks, especially with the ones who keep their handbags tightly closed and who bank their expenses. But this is odd. I tried to telephone the man who kindly arranged the trip for me and was told he was out of the office. He was in court, I was told. Oh dear, what had he done? Nothing. He is a magistrate. It's unbelievable, isn't it? They're everywhere. There's no escape. My milkman is probably a Special Branch man and for all I know the cleaning lady might be a lunatic lifer sprung by Lord Longford for the Christmas hols.

Anyway, should the police or anyone else wish me to help them with their various enquiries, I shall be at the Hotel Grand, Kerkenna, Tunisia until 2 November. And if it isn't grand we shall somehow make it so. By the way, do you think they'll search Dancing Brave when he gets back from California next week? He'll have an awful lot of money on him.

Out to Lunch

8 November 1986

Towards the end of my stay in Kerkenna the hotel manager, who is also the mayor of the island, seemed to think that I was a VIP. God knows why, since I am so shy and retiring, not to say comatose. He drove me to the ferry – he half owns the shipping line too – and took me up to the bridge for the crossing, away from the well of the ship teeming with Arab fishermen and farmers who take their wares to Sfax most days. The crew of the ferry don't bother with uniforms. The captain wore a leather jacket, chewed on a cigar, looked like Pedro Armendariz, and the crew too looked as though they had been leased by Warner Brothers c. 1946. When we docked I was surprised to find that the hotel manager had laid on a car for me with driver to take me all the way to Monastir airport. He had put both car and driver at my disposal for the entire day. The driver, called Sfaxi, said, 'You are to do with me what you will.' We stopped at a few bars on the way to lunch at Sousse and although he was a Moslem he said it was all right for him to have just the one because he felt sure that God was looking the other way that day. We had a pretty hefty lunch in Sousse which set me back all of £4. There is a very good salad in Tunisia called *mechouia* which is a mixture of tomatoes, mild green peppers, chillies, onions and garlic all grilled then peeled and *minced* with caraway seeds, olive oil and lemon juice. But I didn't like their wine much although good manners forced me to persevere with it.

The hotel manager gave me an odd guide book. Under the heading 'Helpful Hints' it says, 'Never lose your temper with the hotel staff, always smile, always look as if you need help – result, instant affection.' Tunisian understatement. I did venture to smile at a waiter one evening and I always need help. Result? He spent half an hour brushing a breadcrumb from one of my succulent thighs. He turned out to be mad. He told me, in French of course, that he had once spent ten days in Liverpool and that he thought it a very wonderful city. He would probably simply adore Belfast. And speaking of Liverpool it is extraordinary how that name or the name Ian Rush can open doors for you abroad. As Tom Baker pointed out to me when I came home you can work your way across Europe by simply smiling and saying things like, 'Manchester United. Very good, yes?' It is best done with a silly Italian accent like Chico Marx's. Then they'll do anything for you.

Anyway it's been all go. As soon as I got back I went to Berlin the following day. Yes, a day trip to Berlin. I know people who used to make frequent trips to Berlin some 40-odd years ago but it does seem rather a long way to go for lunch. I don't agree with this business of us and the Germans being so alike. I find their addiction to sausages, beer and transvestism to be very foreign. They are also very keen on 'gay' jokes and I don't see that homosexuality is any funnier than heterosexuality. They probably do though because there is slightly more chance of being humiliated if you happen to be queer. But after Berlin I shall never again go on a freebie in a group of journalists. It is essential to be a snob about some things and I simply cannot afford to be seen with teenage girls who work for women's magazines or grown men who report for the *Sun* and who should know better. What do they *report* for the *Sun*? Also, gay readers of the *Spectator* will be pleased to know that they were well and fairly represented in Berlin by four correspondents from two gay magazines or papers. Also, there was a man I think from *Time Out* to represent the pot-smoking, Marxist, puritan ethic. I was representing you, whatever that means, and what a bunch of absolute sweeties you are. Home after ten days and I find so many lovely letters from you concerning my legal trials and tribulations. Sitting here with Monica, the dreaded typewriter, I feel as though I'm writing to friends. And it's like old times again. This morning I had to wipe some cauliflower cheese off Monica's keys. Another home-life mystery.

End of an Era

15 November 1986

There is far too much nonsense written about alcohol abuse but nobody seems to give a damn about the abuse of alcoholics. Successive governments have wantonly thrown people on to the streets at 3 p.m. and 11 p.m. daily and the Sunday hours are quite simply sadistic and stupid too. Britain is rapidly becoming a no-smoking area. Sexual intercourse is finished thanks to a drunken sailor and a Haitian pig and there is a licensed drought for 14½ hours every day. For six of those hours I sleep – not easily I can tell you – and I work, or at least think about it, for the odd half hour. That leaves six hours in which to shave and make a cup of tea. Contemplation of the situation has decided me to go off to look for somewhere to die, as I believe elephants do when life gets them down. I don't want to die at home because it could be days before I was found and

I don't want to die in captivity i.e. the Middlesex Hospital. A very nice Indian chef, Ali, dropped dead in the Coach and Horses two years ago and there are very few people in there you would want giving you the kiss of life I can tell you. The man who did attempt it on that occasion always had cold soup in his beard. Anyway, Norman wouldn't like it on the grounds that you *can* take it with you – what's in your pocket at the time that is. But at least somebody had the sense to put what remained of Ali's drink into the ullage. I sometimes think of the customers in there as being a team, if you see what I mean.

But enough. Just a minute ago, someone telephoned to tell me that Sir Gordon Richards is dead. He was the best friend the punters ever had. Unlike Fred Archer and Lester Piggott, whose families were steeped in racing, Gordon Richards was the son of a Shropshire coal-miner. He was born in 1904 and rode in public for the first time in 1920. He became champion jockey for the first time in 1925 with 118 winning mounts. On 4 and 5 October 1933 at Chepstow he achieved the incredible. He rode 11 consecutive winners, six on the first day and then the first five on the second day. In all, between 1920 and 1954, his total number of mounts was 21,834 and his total number of winners was 4,870. The figures are staggering. Statistics may bore some but they tell the story as clearly as does Don Bradman's Test Match batting average of 99.9. On 8 November 1933 he beat Fred Archer's record of 246 winners in a season set up in 1885. The Speaker of the House of Commons said in a reference to him, 'It would be a bad thing to eliminate sentiment from English life. It is just that sentiment which springs from the knowledge that men may rise from humble beginnings and humble birth to big places which affords hope for our country, the hope that everyone may have a chance.'

What makes Gordon Richards's achievements on the Turf so stupendous is the fact that he was riding against the likes of Harry Wragg, Charlie Smirke, Steve Donoghue, Brownie Carslake and Charlie Elliot. How many winners would he have ridden had there been evening racing in his day? He was a very quiet, shy and retiring man, but he was a good raconteur when he got going. I only met him once. It was in Barbados and someone took me over to where he was staying for supper. After, we sat by the beach sipping rum punches and he talked into the night. He also rode the winner of the first horse race

I ever saw at Alexandra Park when I was still a schoolboy. He helped to get me hooked on racing but I don't think that was a bad thing. He once said, 'There is something of racing in the British character, and when you are in racing as I am, you feel very much part of the country and of the community. As far as I am concerned racing is a form of public life. Once you are in that, you never want to get out of it.' He was most likely the *straightest* jockey ever to climb aboard a racehorse and probably made fewer mistakes than any other. It's like the end of an era.

Turning Nasty

29 November 1986

I think it might be a good idea for Mike Tyson to get himself a little cottage in the country with roses around the door and put his feet up before he kills someone. Never before can there have been a true champion of the world in so far as it being inconceivable that he could be beaten by some unknown giant lurking somewhere between Siberia and either Capes Horn or Good Hope. The world secretes hundreds of men in the Jack Dempsey mould – miners, farmhands, navvies and cowboys – who could knock seven kinds of shit out of ordinary champions, but Tyson seems frighteningly different. I now think that Edith Summerskill had it right all along and I've been a devoted fight fan since I was knee high to Jimmy Wilde. Ban it. If it hadn't been for the emergence of Muhammad Ali it wouldn't have been necessary to consider it. Boxing was dying a natural death but he revitalized it with his unique kind of magic. But now it is no longer a noble art, jolly fisticuffs between the fancy or a rousing bar-room brawl and punch-up. It is plain *nasty*. As unpleasant as bear-baiting. Tyson is awesome as is the ocean.

We need a substitute for boxing. Something a little more refined. Personally, I would like to brush-up on my fencing and see duelling reintroduced. The idea of eliminating, say, the Arts Council one by one on consecutive mornings at dawn in Hyde Park appeals to me tremendously. While we're at it we should consider banning soccer. Sports fans reflect the sport they love. We all know about football hooligans but boxing fans are really ghastly too. 'Kill 'im. Kill 'im.' They should be made to try it for themselves, but most of them wouldn't have the guts to get into the ring with Dale Spender, the featherweight champion of the Groucho Club. The grotesque sight of Berbick fumbling for consciousness in that ring last week had the fans almost coming with pleasure.

But perhaps it will soon be unnecessary to consider banning boxing. People will be getting a surfeit of the *Schadenfreude* they crave when AIDS really surfaces like the monster from the deep. There is little point in saying, or writing as Auberon Waugh did, that we mustn't mention it again because it is rapidly replacing the weather as a topic of conversation. As a matter of fact I can't stop wondering whether I might have it or not. Well, what have you been doing over the past five or six years? Or rather who? Although my promiscuous days ended in 1978, the sainted year of my last marriage, I have dabbled a little and a woman has to be pretty promiscuous to go to bed with a rat-bag. Have I since that marriage ended unknowingly been to bed with a fag hag? It's an uncomfortable proposition. No, it's all going to be very different for those of us who survive. Never mind boxing. When they finally ban smoking and then drinking we'll be having friends round for muesli evenings. And those expense lunches will be fun. 'What would you like sir?' 'I'll start with the shredded wheat and skimmed milk and then I'll have the dried apricot with a hazel nut.' 'I'm afraid the apricot will take 20 minutes sir. You see we have to dig it out of the compost.' 'Oh, that's all right. We'll jog around the block while we're waiting.' And we must take a last lingering look at children. People won't be making many of them any more. The daily battle against melancholy is going to get harder. Even with one foot in the grave and a banana skin behind me it is amazing to me that some of us keep winning. I'm deeply suspicious of the current cheerfulness. In fact I said to Irma last week that I was considering consulting a psychiatrist to find out just why it is that my pecker is up.

But something is bound to turn up to put me in touch with reality again. And it just has. I have to find somewhere new to live. Investigations I have carried out over the past two days lead me to believe that anyone can get a flat in London if they have a mere £100,000. So that's all right. What I dread most about moving is finding what's been under the bed for the past six years. An unwritten book, an odd sock and a mummified scrubber I shouldn't wonder. Meanwhile, today is brand new and I just know something wonderful will turn up.

Dangerous Ladies *13 December 1986*

Those foolish young men, members of the Dangerous Sports Club, who jump off the Clifton Suspension Bridge on the end of elastic ropes and who try the Cresta Run blindfolded or drunk or both, don't know the half of it when it comes to real danger. I do. I once had an affair with a girl who worked for *Spare Rib*. On another occasion, while becalmed on this voyage to the grave, I got the wind up by going out with a woman who worked for *Cosmopolitan* magazine. The subsequent nervous twitching on the right hand side of my face plus the grey hair are the result of domestic shellshock. The woman on *Cosmo* had all black eyes, no iris all pupil, so intense was her single-minded ambition. And what, you may ask, did she think she could get out of this tired sack? Well, would you believe it, she thought I could introduce her to famous people. I suppose I could have done but I wonder just what the hell she thought the likes of Lester Piggott could do for a hack virago.

With seriously dangerous women you can hear them thinking in the dark. Something you did or didn't do the day before festers and it's like fermentation. And I don't like suddenly being whacked in the dark. They should put the bedside light on before throwing a punch. The first woman from that mould I ever met was the matron of my last prep school, the dreaded Mrs Spencer-Payne. I was wetting the bed quite a lot then and whenever I did she used to slap me across the face really hard. Of course that only escalated the bed-wetting so then, after we had queued up for our tablespoon of malt – do they still make it? – she'd whack me over the head with the spoon. Looking back on it, I suppose she didn't much like small boys. I can see her point now but it was all rather alarming then. There was also a mistress who taught French and not a lot got learned. She distracted me, being as she was something of a knockout. When she walked past my desk I would drop a pencil on the floor in the hope that I would be able to look up her skirt when

I bent down to pick it up. At first she thought I was plain clumsy. Then she twigged and hit me over the head with a fairly ample dictionary. My French has been lousy ever since.

In those days I thought that all women must be like school-mistresses, plain nasty and dangerous, but it wasn't until the first time that I fell in love that I realized that most of them are mad as well. The object of that love and lust actually stabbed me. Only in the arm but it was extremely painful. So I moved out of that pad and got myself a bedsitter in Queen's Gate. The landlady there was a Pole and she was full of menace like distant thunder. I never got caught taking girls back – strictly against house rules after 10 p.m. as if you couldn't do the deed in daylight – but another tenant did and as he left the house she dropped a chamber pot on him from the second floor. If it hadn't just missed it probably would have killed him. It was time to move again. The next landlady was a hideous thing called Mrs Shillibeer. Late one night, feeling rather frustrated about something or other, probably the other, I punched a hole through the plywood door of my wardrobe. She fetched the police. That was my first meeting with them although my mother had threatened me with them when I was about 12 for putting bangers through neighbours' letter boxes. (I drew the line at putting them into empty milk bottles as my chum did.) So I had to move again.

God knows how many landladies I had when I was a teenager but I lived in dread of them. The word landlady still gives me a shudder and the powers that be could well name a nuclear deterrent the Landlady. I used to place objects in my bed-sitters in very precise positions before going out to work or play and I would find that they had invariably been moved when I returned. They snooped around like dogs. I wouldn't know now, thank God, but I suppose they have changed with the times. They probably chuck you out now if you don't bring a girl back at midnight. I would be homeless. I wouldn't know what to do with a girl now at that time of day.

Trick or Treat

20/27 December 1986

I don't think about it very often but I did once kill someone with kindness you might say. It was in 1971. I was writing a twice-weekly column for the *Sporting Life*. (Stop me if you've heard this.) I was loafing around in the office one afternoon when the editor summoned me to tell me that Ras Prince Monolulu of 'I've gotta horse' fame was seriously ill in the Middlesex Hospital. Didn't I think it would be a good idea to go and visit the old boy and maybe write a piece about him? Yes. So off I went pausing on the way to buy him a box of chocolates. It wasn't until I arrived at his bedside that I realized I had inadvertently bought him Black Magic. Luckily he didn't notice. He was in a pretty feeble state but he mustered a smile and asked after a horse or two. He whispered about this and that and then I opened the Black Magic. He opted for the strawberry cream which I located on the map and then popped into his vacant mouth. He bit on it and then coughed. Then he coughed again and again and again. Just as I was becoming slightly irritated by all this coughing I suddenly realized that he was choking and at that moment the ward sister bustled over. She sat him up, slapped his back, told me to leave at once and drew the screens around him. I didn't think all that much about it until the next day when I read in the morning paper that he was dead. It is extraordinary to me to think that a strawberry cream could be an offensive weapon never mind a coup de grâce. The fact that he was dying anyway is neither here nor there. Without that old Black Magic he might at least have lingered on for long enough to have got the result of the St Leger.

I was reminded of all that yesterday when Norman actually *gave* me a smoked salmon sandwich in the bar. He said the salmon came from the same shop that he gets it from to give me whenever I'm in the Middlesex Hospital. There but for the grace of God. You can't be too careful and all that. But a strawberry cream is food for thought. It makes me wonder how many times I must have been on the brink of death in hospital only to have been saved by the greed of my visitors who always eat all my grapes. (They talk amongst themselves too and never to me.) Yes, he was a nice old chap. Monolulu, and people like the old Aga Khan wouldn't have put up with him if he hadn't been. He was a pretty shrewd nut too and he had a flat in Wigmore Street to prove it. But I wonder what was given as the cause of death on his death certificate. Not the *Sporting Life* I hope.

The only other time I might have killed someone was 20 years ago when I lived in Suffolk. The old witch who owned my cottage had a filthy mongrel who used to keep trotting up the road and attempt the legover with my delightful labrador bitch called Smedley. I got very fed up with this and late one night while having just the one in the Peacock I decided to shoot her. Not Smedley, Mrs Petch, for that was her name. Luckily, for Mrs Petch and my freedom, somebody telephoned my then wife and told her to hide my shotgun, which she did in among the lupins. At the time I think I meant it. Anyway, I borrowed an air rifle shortly after that ghastly night and posted myself at the bedroom window and waited for the Petch dog. I got him in the arse and he must have thought it was a hornet. I never saw him again. But what a good shotgun that was. It was a Cogswell and Harrison 12-bore given to me by Michael Nelson who wrote *A Room in Chelsea Square* and another man not to be trusted with firearms. A couple of years later, when things were desperate, I brought it to London where I sold it to a man over lunch in the Trattoria Terrazza for £30. Fool. I then put £25 of that on a horse which duly got stuffed. That was quite a bet considering we were ekeing out the continuing stew and whisky on £15 a week. Anyway, they're terrible things guns. They let me fire nearly every weapon in the army when I went to Sandhurst to write about the place. After a few minutes on the range I got a little bored and found myself half wishing that the targets were people and not cards. What I should have done was give the Petch dog a strawberry cream. Poisoned, of course.

In the Lion's Den

3 January 1987

I was walking along Cleveland Street the other day in a cold drizzle when I suddenly came across an amazing collage on the pavement which just about summed up the human condition to perfection. It comprised a pool of vomit, an empty beer can, some dog shit and a sprinkling of confetti. I am not a squeamish man and I expect people who drink beer to vomit from time to time and allow their dogs to foul the pavement but there was something so stark about the confetti that it has been in and on my mind ever since. I could stuff a pillow with the amount of confetti I have had thrown at me. And could I sleep easily on that? No. The resultant depression was heightened by walking on past the Middlesex Hospital and so I quickened the feeble steps toward the analgesic. They were unlocking the doors as I arrived and there's a mystery. The timing is extraordinary. Take an instance a few weeks ago. I was in Birmingham and caught a train to London. Not a particular train, simply the next one. I got to Euston and then got into a taxi to go to the pub. I arrived as they were unlocking the doors. That wasn't planned but an SS panzer division couldn't have been more precise. Odd, isn't it? I reckon if I set out to walk to Basingstoke or Fort William it would be opening time when I arrived. But of course I wouldn't walk for fear of tripping over the confetti on the way. Why do we do it? Dogs may foul the pavement but they don't presume to get married. Anyway, the analgesic took a long time to work because there was another shock horror awaiting in the pub in the form of a newspaper which informed me that the President of the USA is about to have prostate surgery and that one of his right-hand men has had a brain tumour. These people have their fingers on the button. I wouldn't be at all surprised to learn that the lawns of the White House are covered with pools of vomit, empty beer cans, dog shit and confetti.

But, thanks be to heaven, the day had a happy ending. I went to a party given by the CID. I think it rather strange that the people who have arrested me thrice should invite me for

Christmas cocktails. What worried me was that I might get arrested again in the middle of the party for being drunk. But I kept my head and all was well. And a funny thing happened on my way to midnight. I found myself sitting next to a charming lady detective and what surprised me was that it aroused strange feelings of masochism that I didn't really think were within me. I know quite well that it is masochistic to eat in the Coach and Horses and to back two-year-olds first time out but I didn't think I was masochistic about women. The first time I was bombarded with confetti was a clue I didn't spot. Brain damage and I don't even work for Mr Reagan. Anyway, when I eventually left the police party I took the wrong overcoat. The next day I telephoned Vine Street nick and told them so. The man I spoke to asked me if the overcoat I had taken was better than mine and I told him yes, it was cashmere and mine was mere Crombie. To my amazement he then said, 'Well, I should hang on to it if I were you.' Of course, I didn't. I don't want police dogs shitting all over my carpet. Lord Longford is the greatest deterrent since Pierrepoint hung up his rope. And also I think the lady detective might have had a gun in her handbag.

There may be more frightening things than detectives though. As I write to you I am about to depart to the sticks for the Christmas follies and I shall be staying with two women. Two. One of them is a doctor and the other is an agony aunt. Could this be a case of killing two birds with one stoned? A policeman's ball and now this. It's like living in a lion's den. This morning a Christmas card arrived wishing me a merry time and all that and also a PS asking for £25 each way on Legal Bid for the Derby. I really must put an ad in all the papers including the *Police Gazette* saying I don't take bets any more. But should a two-year-old appear called either Collage or Confetti this year then we will be in business again.

Down by the Riverside

10 January 1987

I went back to Lambourn last weekend and it still possesses characteristics that are really heartwarming. Apart from the racehorses and the small people who look after them there are one or two good men who deserve to be mentioned in dispatches from the front line of the fight against ASH, Action on Alcohol Abuse, jogging, health food and anything else that is destroying the fibre of this once great country. Irish Tom excelled himself on Saturday night. He had just the 15 or so and won £400 at pool and spoof. At closing time he decided to walk home and just before he reached it he felt a sudden and agonizing necessity to evacuate his enraged bowels. As he was walking along the banks of the River Lambourn he thought what better place and so walked into the water. Once he negotiated mid-stream he began to undress. Lesser men would have simply lowered their trousers but Tom is very fussy for an Irishman. He wanted to do a proper job. So first he removed his shoes and one can only imagine that to be quite difficult in a river at night after just the one never mind 15. He then took his trousers right off and did his business. While that was being transacted his trousers, with the £400 in the pockets, floated off down the river. I spent all morning up until opening time the next day on the river bank between his house and the pub looking for them. I hoped that they might have been snarled up on a rock or a weeping willow but no such luck. They are probably in Newbury by now and heading for the Thames.

I think you will now understand the high regard in which I hold Tom. What I do wonder about though is what his wife's reaction was at being confronted by a very wet man naked from the waist down apart from his socks which were probably full of tiddlers as well as feet. I don't think in the circumstances an explanation was required. I certainly couldn't think of an *excuse* which is what a wife wants to hear. At a lunch party the following day I noticed that she didn't laugh at a single one of his rather good jokes. She may, of course, have memorized his repertoire after 25 years of marriage but she most likely deduced from his midnight appearance that he had been to a public house. But there are not enough men like Tom and we desperately need reinforcements. And gentlemen in England then a-bed when Tom had his tom tit shall think themselves accursed they were not there. Hopefully.

The river along the valley is very pretty and it attracts all sorts. It may well be a Lambourn Triangle. When I lived there with my fourth, last, most sainted and angry wife there was a bloodstock agent who drove deliberately into the river in his fairly posh car. He said it was a warm and humid summer's evening and he simply wanted to cool off. You know it makes sense. It is a useful river too. A vet from West Ilsley once gave me the skull of an ex-Grand National winner that subsequently broke his back in a race at Newbury. He had boiled it but when he gave it to me in a sack it was still pretty gungy and smelled awful. We put it in the river and left it there for two or three weeks. The worms did their job and when we pulled it out it was shining white like polished ivory. It was an extraordinary objet d'art on our mantelshelf until I went mad and gave it away. Then there was the time when a traveller in the Swan at Shefford asked the guvnor if there were any fish in the river. He replied that yes there were and threw a line out of the dining-room window which overlooks the river. In less than a minute he hauled in a trout. I suppose those lunatics the animal rights activists would have burned the pub down had they been around. And there was the obligatory pub bore – handyman, poacher, ex-Desert Rat, you name it – who amazingly stitched up some American tourists one day. He told them that the river was so full of trout that he didn't need a rod and line. He told them he just used to put a frying pan on the bank and the trout would jump into it. We were not told whether there was a fire under the pan and butter in it at the time but the Americans swallowed it hook, line and sinker. Yes, it would be lovely to live by a river. So soothing and water lilies are my favourite flowers, but we must buy Tom a life-jacket.

Mein Kampf

17 January 1987

I have just had to bale out of Berlin where I have been attempting a magazine piece on the wretched place. We should have waited until the spring. It was 20 degrees below when I arrived there last Sunday and still slowly dropping when I telephoned my doctor who confirmed that I was mad and said go home and stay there. The only good thing to have come out of this weather is the fact that it has replaced AIDS at the top of the topics of conversation chart. But it was impossible to see anything in Berlin to write home about. You don't get the feel of a place if you're wearing glasses in a blizzard. So I spent most of the time sitting in a very good cafe reminiscent of one or two I know in Greenwich Village. There was evidence to suggest that it may be a rendezvous point for Baader-Meinhof terrorists. There was piped classical music – all the Vivaldi that any student could wish for and very nice too – very hard-looking women accompanied by dirty and aggressive babies and a lot of men who looked like Lenin and who seemed to be drawing plans on odd pieces of paper at their tables.

The babies were really dreadful, though, and I've had them up to here. Mothers should deposit them in the cloakroom when they come into cafés and restaurants and they are awful on aeroplanes too, where they should be put into the luggage compartments for the duration. All the babies I have seen since winter arrived are dressed up to look like bunny rabbits with runny noses. Of course they shouldn't be allowed out until they are 16 years old and then only for very short bursts. I also resent being hypnotized by their oral activities. As soon as they open their mouths their mothers put something into them. Almost anything will be accepted as long as it is sticky or made of rubber. They're like little pedal bins. You just wiggle a toe or a finger and hey presto they open their mouths. And speaking of mouths, don't those Germans keep shoving food into theirs? I found the helpings in restaurants hugely off-putting. I ordered pork chops in one place and got half a pig. But the Germans are waging a great counter-offensive against the ASH people. As far as I could see they are chain smokers to a man. (A friend of mine who came over here as a refugee in the 1930s tells me that the Storm Troopers were useful to small boys who collected cigarette cards. How nice.)

Anyway, a wasted three days in Berlin and for nothing. I couldn't even find Norman – whose birthday it was the day I came home – a picture postcard of Hitler. His sense of humour is sometimes a trifle perverse for a Jew. Now, here he is after 60 glorious years. His old mum, unaware of what she was saying, told me, 'Yes, I'll never forget the day Norman was born. It was Friday the 13th.' Say no more. But she did. She went on to tell me what a good little boy he was. It's a disgusting thought. I wonder at what age he developed the devilish cunning that enabled him to find a catering shop that sells dinner plates that have a diameter one inch less than the standard ones used in most restaurants. At least he has taken to buying drinks now that he is famous. The change that has come over him is fascinating to watch. When I met him first he was a depressive. After a bit of publicity he became a manic depressive and now he is a paranoid manic depressive. Waving a copy of this or some other magazine at his customers the other day he walked up and down the bar shouting, 'I'm immortal. I'm immortal.' I sometimes look at him and think that we hacks have created a monster whom we can no longer control. He, poor fool, sees it the other way round.

Girl-talk

31 January 1987

If you want a mind-blowing experience that makes Dale Spender look like Marilyn Monroe or the *Guardian* read like *Tit-Bits* then you should read a book called *Pornography* written by a nut called Andrea Dworkin. Fred Ingrams gave it to me with his tongue in his cheek and a healthy smirk on his face. It is on the usual subject of what pigs men are and, no surprise, it is written by an American. It really gives me the horrors sometimes to sit here and wonder at the amount of hate that there is out there. You get inklings of it when you write a column and occasionally receive mad letters from crazy readers, but women like Andrea Dworkin are something else. They must be contorted and ulcerated with hate. The proposition that all men despise women is just bollocks. Mind you, it isn't difficult to despise the loony feminists like Andrea Dworkin but I promise you that it has nothing to do with the fact that they are all physically repulsive to a man. I also very much object to being told on which course my libido should be set. Women are sex objects for me because I am a male heterosexual. Were I a chair I should fancy a table.

Ms Dworkin is also revolted by what is called the missionary position but she doesn't give us a better one. She should look at animals. In my experience, given the dominant position, women don't do terribly well. Why should they? Why write a bloody book about it? Why write a column about it? Well, I'll tell you why, it is because I have been distracted from all else since a snotty-nosed window-cleaner knocked my copy of Dworkin's venom on to the floor. At this very minute the little git is standing on my desk and has actually had the cheek to rest one of his filthy cloths on my bust of Nelson. Having just informed me that he is off to Sandown Park next week for the day – the greatest event yet in his 19 years – I asked him, with Andrea Dworkin in mind, if he liked girls. He tells me that they are smashing. I then advised him that it might show disrespect, loathing and sadistic tendencies on his part were he to mount his girlfriend according to the gospel of daffy Dworkin. 'Let her get on top of you.' I told him. He replied, 'We've tried that and she doesn't like it that way and she thinks it's rude.' Quite so. I would very much like to be the fly on the wall and see this healthy young man clean Dworkin's windows but I value his life more than the monthly £10 I give him. Not that she'd kill him, quite the reverse if anything, but they write their books very high up in New York. Here he has only to fall a mere three floors. As a man who is terrified of heights I asked him idly was he? Surprisingly he told me that he too was terrified. So why be a window-cleaner I asked him. 'It's my dad. He's the boss and he makes me do it.' Dad, I have noticed, always cleans only the insides of the windows whereas the likely lad goes out on to the ledges. It's rather Dickensian really. I think he'd go up my chimney if I asked him nicely.

Which reminds me, what's happened to my friend Clive? He maintains that any woman will go to bed with you if you ask her nicely. I wonder would Andrea Dworkin? I suppose she might if you said that you were doing it for research for the Institute of Advanced Studies at Princeton University. It is awful to think that had she been passing Glen Oak Farm five years ago and persuaded Navajo Princess to mount Lyphard we would have had no Dancing Brave. We decent chaps can't abide male chauvinist pigs but we must be grateful that stallions totally despise brood mares. Otherwise our window-cleaner would have absolutely nothing to see at Sandown Park next week. And now, a moment ago, he peered at a photograph on the wall of one of my ex-wives and asked me, 'Is that Gayle Hunnicut?' No, it wasn't you Sue, or you Jill, it was Jacki. Now, do I look like a missionary that Gayle Hunnicut would ever have gone into the jungle with? I ask you. This boy needs to do some homework and I think he should be taken into Soho to get a real feel of the ring before the fight starts. And I suppose that Dworkin would say cleaning windows is an act of aggression too. You must have to despise a window to wipe it.

Bobbing and Weaving

28 February 1987

The postman has got a terrific feeling for montage. Yesterday he delivered a letter from the House of Lords inviting me to a party in the House of Commons and another from the Bloomsbury and Marylebone County Court informing me that they have issued a warrant for my arrest for contempt. They go on to say that if I fail to appear on 4 March then I shall be imprisoned. It's funny that because it is the same day as the cocktail party in the Commons and it is also my daughter's 17th birthday. What a busy day. There are also two race meetings at Wetherby and Worcester. It is the sort of day that puts it all into a nutshell. To get the full benefit out of 4 March I think I will try and arrange a working breakfast with somebody at the Connaught. I like a flying start.

But I have no contempt for the County Court. Far from it. I think they do a wonderful job. They even put yellow ink over the words 'arrest' and 'imprisonment' on the warrant just in case my adrenalin glands need waking up. Yes, I'm being sued by a dentist. I could have paid him ages ago but I have been reluctant to fork out £100 for a temporary filling. It seems a lot for putting a bit of cotton wool into a hole. Now, with £46 costs added to the bill my petulance has cost me the price of a ploughman's lunch plus 125 large vodkas to wash it down with. Or the return air fare to Dublin where a publican has invited me to stay with him. Does he want to kill me?

So the next day the relentless postman brought me a postcard from Irma Kurtz who seems to be in Washington in the company of three raccoons, plus a smashing bill from the Inland Revenue. But I have cracked the Inland Revenue at last. I said to a mate on the *Sunday Express*, the brilliant Graham Lord, 'Look at this demand. What the hell shall I do?' He said, 'Pay it.' That is fantastic and so simplistic. It has never occurred to me before that you can get these people off your back by paying up. For years I have been bobbing and weaving, ducking and diving, and all along I could have simply paid up on the dot. I think life is going to become a lot smoother from here on in. I am very grateful to Graham for that advice. With him around who needs an accountant?

I was going to spend the money on furniture for my new flat but you don't need more than a bed, a typewriter and a corkscrew. But I did get some very silly advice from a woman reader of the *Sunday Mirror* who wrote to me to tell me that I could furnish a flat from jumble sales. I don't know what sort of people she thinks work for Mirror Group Newspapers but I could tell her that the printers go to Le Gavroche for their tea breaks. Well, the dentist and the Inland Revenue now put firmly in their places we can put our feet up and write a book. Come to think of it I can't unless I can find a desk in a jumble sale. Perhaps the Distressed Gentlefolk people have jumble sales where you can find useful things like old pith helmets, maid's uniforms, stuffed owls, collections of Not Wanted On Voyage labels, gaiters, tea cosies, croquet hoops, old Afghan War medals and desks. What an extraordinary flat it is going to be. And think of the shame and embarrassment it will cause my brothers and daughter when I am found dead dressed in a maid's uniform and wearing a VC. That, by the way, is one of the bonuses of being permanently in debt. You can't lie about rotting because these Inland Revenue and VAT people have a penchant for breaking down doors. I don't want to go in a dustbin liner.

If only friends were as punctilious as bailiffs about keeping in touch. It says quite a lot about someone as to how long they could be dead before being found. I read somewhere once that a man had died over his pint of beer in the corner of a pub early one evening and they never noticed until chucking-out time. I've known and do know some pub bores but he must have been the guvnor of them all. You'd think somebody might have asked him for a light or whether he'd care to make up a four at darts. I wonder too whether they put his beer back into the ullage. If he had got it on the slate they probably did. But what with VAT on coffins we must hang on and deny the bastards.

Guinness and Mash

28 March 1987

Now that flat racing is with us again we born-again losers will shortly become reacquainted with the agony of victory and the thrill of defeat. I hope to see Framlington Park win the William Hill Lincoln Handicap today, although at the moment I don't know where he is drawn. Norman and the Groucho Club need the money and the trainer, Peter Walwyn, is a very decent man. Unfortunately the wizards at *Timeform* label the horse as being inconsistent. Who isn't?

But spring is in the air and I bought a pair of binoculars this week which will doubtless be lost in some members' bar between York and Brighton before the Derby. It is amazing the number of pairs of bins I have lost in bars and on trains since 1970. And, sad to say, we have also lost the man who supplied us with cheap caviare on the racecourse. Where he got it from was a mystery I never tried to solve. There are some things the world is not yet ready to know, as Dr Watson was fond of saying.

But it will be good to see the 'faces' at the races again, even those of some really rather awful people, even the bookmaker who has the dreadful habit of addressing me as 'young man'. That's so bloody rude and patronizing and I don't need reassurances about my age and appearance. There's a stall-holder in Berwick Street market I have stopped shopping with because he uses the phrase. Speak standard English and they think you are an idiot. When he says, 'How about some lovely fennel, young man?' I know he is thinking, 'Cor blimey, it's that bleary-eyed prick again. Expect he's a poof.'

Yes, it is high time the myth of the lovable cockney was exposed. It probably started with Shaw's Henry Higgins. Maybe Kipling. And what has kept the myth going is that so many middle-class people think it rather smart, engaging and amusing to have a working-class acquaintance. I could point you to a man with a stall who would punch you in the mouth if you touched an avocado to test it for ripeness.

There's a lot of it in the country too where every village has its cracker-barrel philosopher who bores the arse off you. Me anyway. Any day now somebody is going to tell me what his man at the garage thinks is going to win the 2,000 Guineas. I only welcome suggestions from people professionally involved in racing and I didn't get where I am today by listening to my barber, milkman, or the lunatic in the off-licence. And now, sitting here in the gutter, I wonder if I should have done.

Of course, as we all know, jockeys are the worst tipsters. When they start talking to me I feel I should tie myself to the mast, as it were. I will also back anything tipped to me by an Irish trainer. Mick O'Toole was a butcher then a greyhound trainer before he took to racehorses and he kindly took me to the dogs in Dublin one night. He really knows his dogs. We backed eight consecutive losers that night and he had to lend me the money to pay for my hotel. Well, he didn't *have* to. Then at the Curragh he took me to a pub that Pat Eddery's father ran, one Sunday lunchtime for the one. He really meant just the one and implied that his wife might assault him if we were late back and spoiled the lunch. We left that pub the following afternoon. He's a good man and a fearless punter. I was looking at a horse in his yard once and ventured that he could probably stay pretty well. Mick turned round and said, 'He couldn't stay seven furlongs in a fucking horse-box.'

I shall go back to Dublin at the earliest opportunity. People keep saying how dreadfully expensive it is, which I know, but they will keep using a pint of Guinness as a yardstick by which to measure the cost of living. I don't really give a damn about the cost of Guinness and I dread being given it on the National Health when I end up in an old people's home.

Which reminds me, I am told that there is an obscure renal disease which necessitates shots of gin. But I suppose the stuff really must be good for you. They used to give Arkle two pints of Guinness a day with his mash and six raw eggs, and he could jump a bit. I just hope that Framlington Park finished up all his greens and pudding last night.

Oh, Madeleine!

4 April 1987

I have just had a letter from a woman reader in North Yorkshire in which she says some extraordinary things, not least, 'What a wonderful life you've had so far!' You could have fooled me and how on earth can one *possibly* give that impression? It makes me wonder what on earth other people's lives can be like. She says that she lives in the wilds of the magnificent Yorkshire Dales. Well, just you stay there, Madeleine. I was a prince when I first came to Soho aged 15, got kissed and was turned into a toad. It takes all my muscle to refrain from croaking now. But if you think it is a wonderful life propping up bars surrounded by people who used to be something or who were never going to be anything plus listening to Norman's mum telling you how her grandfather opened the first umbrella shop in Gower Street in 1867 and on top of that backing horses like Framlington Court which came in 19th, then you are the only woman in the world not in touch with reality.

There comes a time, Madeleine, when on the occasions that people smile at you, you realize that it isn't because they are glad to see you, it is because they are thinking, 'There but for the grace of God go I.' One is a constant source of consolation to others. And another thing. You ask me the daftest question I have ever been asked, 'What about the *Guardian* – why don't you write for them?' Oh Madeleine, Madeleine. You don't know what you ask but my colleagues in Fleet Street will appreciate that one. You might as well ask a fishwife why she isn't singing *Aida* or *Norma*. Or ask a gelding why he hasn't been entered for the Derby.

Madeleine, you slay me and this calls for a drink. That's better. Oh dear, you must be a strange woman to write, 'Try to keep fit and out of hospital where you seem impelled to throw, or rather hurl, butter about. Was it Lurpak?' What on earth has the make of the butter got to do with it? As a matter of fact it was Anchor which is much harder and therefore more damaging. Appropriate, too, since I compared the target nurse to being like the Santissima Trinidad.

You also ask if I am still writing for the *Spectator*. I'm not sure, my dear. Some would say that I merely relieve myself into my typewriter once a week. And what you say about reading my book is odd too. 'By the end of the book I felt I'd enjoyed every minute with you – especially the frequent Smirnoffs.' How could you? The vodka has to be frequent when you are like a steeple-jack with vertigo. You can't actually like the stuff. It doesn't taste of anything. But to cap it all you say, 'I'm really very envious and begin to feel I've wasted my time up to now.' I find that very moving and touching and quite mad. You mustn't envy, Madeleine, and you haven't wasted your time.

What do you say I come up to Grassington and we give it a whirl? I see myself running to you across the moors, leaping over gambolling lambs and then sweeping you into my arms. I thought I was Heathcliff when I was 12 but later realized what a twit he was. Come to think about it I'm not even sure about the actual running bit or sweeping you up, depending on your weight. But we could go to York races, get drunk in Malton with the jockeys and show our magnificent profiles to the wind that sweeps across those moors. Have you got any money and is there a decent pub in Grassington?

Would you allow me to smoke in bed? Can we have Yorkshire pudding and gravy as a *separate* course to begin with? Say yes. I like my eggs boiled for three minutes and please don't let your whippets sleep on the bed. Our bed. Just think of it. And Madeleine is such a lovely name. I can hear myself whisper it in the dark, shout it exultantly in fields of sun-drenched poppies. This calls for another drink. There. I spoke your name aloud and it was like a caress only comparable to 'They're off'.

How could you think I have had a wonderful life before I received your letter?

Which reminds me, please could you send me a photograph of yourself with an s.a.e. and the fare to Grassington. Bear up my love, it won't be long. To have discovered you, the purpose of my being, calls for another drink. That's better. PS. Please put on a heavy Yorkshire accent if you haven't got one. It turns me on.

Lemon Roux

11 April 1987

After having tipped you the horse that finished 19th in the William Hill Lincoln Handicap, Framlington Court, I felt I had lost all credibility. A pity about that because I felt pretty sure that Maori Venture would win the Seagram Grand National which he duly did at no less than 28–1. Not only did he jump Aintree that afternoon he jumped out of the pages of my form books and newspapers and right into my eyes every time I saw his name. It was so strong a hunch that it had my guts aching. Unfortunately it was one of those rare days when I decided to be sensible and that is something that hardly ever pays off.

Just before I telephoned Victor Chandler I caught sight of myself in a mirror and I lingered in front of it for a moment and thought yes you are a twit and you need all sorts of boring things like new clothes, furniture for the impending but evasive flat, teeth fixed, bills paid and safari porters for yet another expedition to find Miss Right. So I just had a fiver each way. I'd be kicking myself still if I wasn't too weak. Always follow your instincts. Of course gamblers are rarely contented and I felt almost gloomy as I watched the horse draw away in the final furlong. Babies invariably want more sweeties than they are given.

Otherwise it wasn't a bad afternoon. Five friends including a woman who was once daft enough to divorce me came round to watch the race and I cooked them a meal which goes down quite well on such occasions and which came of the Saturday pages of the *Times*. Not a lot comes out of the *Times* now for me apart from Jonathan Meades' 'Eating Out' and George

Robinson, the Newmarket correspondent on the racing page, but this is a good little Greek number. You boil a couple of chickens with tarragon – I boil roasting ones – let them cool and then skin them, bone them and put them in pieces onto a large dish. Over that lot you pour a sauce which is a basic roux but with lemon juice, egg yolks and cream stirred in. It is best served with saffron rice and as readers of this column will know saffron is obtainable from the Old Compton Street delicatessen in exchange for condoms which the hideous proprietor seems to have some use for.

But that dish always reminds me of the strange thing said by the woman who wrote it up in the *Times*, Shona Crawford Poole. I spoke to her on the telephone once and ever so humbly suggested I might write a travel piece for her for those Saturday pages. She said, 'Yes, but first let me see something you've written.' I was flabbergasted and don't get me wrong, not because I think I am something special, but that somebody with any authority on the *Times* should *not* read the *Spectator*. Mind you, I think it is quite extraordinary that *anybody* should not read the *Spectator*. Even the cleaning lady glances at it when she is removing the saffron rice from this typewriter. She is freaked out by 'Home life' and thinks Alice Thomas Ellis is an upper-class charwoman. Well, I suppose she is in a way.

But anyway, I have got a little travel piece to write for a magazine and I am off to Lanzarote for a week. I dread it. Since I accepted the job I have met no less than six people who have been there and they have all said that it is the most boring place on earth. A volcanic ash-heap with Watney's bitter and chips. What is more an airline pilot once told me he dreaded landing there. What a comedown after a 28–1 winner and lunch at Brown's.

It is a self-catering jaunt and I am to have my own villa, a euphemism for bungalow, and my private swimming-pool into which I shall stare all day while not cooking rice. Such a waste on someone who can't swim, thanks to my brother having pushed me into a goldfish pond when I was two and so making me terrified of non-carbonated water. The other bad omen is that Lanzarote, that marvellous Champion Hurdle winner, was killed when he took to jumping fences. Why name a racehorse Lanzarote? Would you call a horse Southend-on-Sea? No. When I told Victor Chandler I was going to Lanzarote he shook his head and smiled sadly as though he had just laid six consecutive winning favourites. And for real money.

Under the Volcano *25 April 1987*

What a feckless, disappointing lot you readers are. Somebody, just one of you, might have had the decency to write to me and warn me off my freebie to Lanzarote. I spent a week drinking my Grand National winnings staring at a wall and wondering just why God decided to create cockroaches. Your average Spanish barman wasn't a particularly brilliant creation either. Nice enough but oh, so slow. And what strange people go to such resorts. The courier who organized this little self-catering trip asked me to meet her in a certain hotel when I arrived. I waited for her for two hours. It transpired that she had been sitting in the lobby all the time and I was ten yards away waiting in the bar. How like a woman. Women don't seem to realize that you need a drink until about two days after you have married them. Then they try and call last orders.

But we met up and had a little chat and then, to my horror, she said, 'Shall I tell you my philosophy of life?' It is an awful moment when somebody announces that they are a bore. 'Please do,' I said. 'Well, life is very short. You've got to be happy because you're not here for long. If you don't like what you are doing, then change because life is very short.' I nodded sagely and sent the waiter a distress signal. 'Yes, life is terribly short,' she said again and again. She told me so many times that I began glancing at my watch to see how much longer I'd got. Never have I felt closer to death. She drove me to a little more than just the one and eventually I crashed out on a sun lounger.

When I woke up, someone had stolen one of my shoes. Just the one. This was not only inconvenient but rather frightening. As an ardent Sherlock Holmes fan I immediately pondered the horrors that befell Sir Henry Baskerville on the Grimpen Mire after the hound had got the scent of one of his shoes which was nicked from a London hotel. But I think in this instance it was stolen by a small boy in the next villa who seemed rather unhappy. He has awful parents. Some parents are the dreadful penalty that children are doomed to pay for their existence. And vice versa.

But what a dump. Have you ever looked into an extinct volcano? It's the nearest you can get to being a proctologist. There are also all-year-round gales on Lanzarote. They blow hot from Africa and can knock you over if you tip the scales at a mere 126 lbs. There is also an excessive amount of Muzak. For one lunch I had the '1812' overture with the starter and then the 'Sugar Plum Fairy' with the chicken and chips. I didn't hear one note of the Spanish music I love in seven days. Why I was eating lunch in a hotel was because I gave up the self-catering business after the second day. I don't much like eating alone in a still, silent room. I like to see the faces even if some of them have to tell me that life is so short.

Then one evening I came across a snake on my little patio which gave me one hell of a fright. I hurled a bottle of mineral water at it and there was broken glass everywhere. It turned out, on closer inspection, to be a twig and not a snake. The couple in the next villa watched all this and shook their heads sadly, thinking me mad. The Spanish waiters spent time shaking their heads sadly too. They are very good character readers. They twig very quickly that you have elected to fight for the legion of the damned, shake their heads, wish they could join you, but HP payments restrict a married man's ambitions so terribly. The local women were nice. There's something rather poignant about watching a woman on her knees scrubbing tiles and I seriously considered giving the one who did for me a subscription to the *Guardian*. But the dogs are strange. I have noticed it before – all Spanish dogs are depressives.

But it wasn't *all* bad. Sitting on the patio in the evening with a long drink and the fallen hibiscus petals swirling around my shoeless foot made a pleasant change from sitting here and staring out of the window into Great Portland Street pondering just how short life may be. I find it a little irritating that she, the Lanzarote philosopher, will almost certainly live to be a hundred. She was plump with stupidity, not happiness.

Party Politics

2 May 1987

Who the hell invented the wine-and-cheese party? It has to be one of the most ghastly functions devised by man since the stag party. It was probably thought up shortly after the war by a Hampstead poet with a subscription to the *New Statesman*. People involved with the Arts Council are in their element at these dos but my idea of a fun evening does not include nibbling bits of rubber cheese, sipping Hirondelle and discussing Mary Wollstonecraft crushed eye to eye with Margaret Drabble or one of the many clones of Claire Tomalin that are to be seen everywhere these days. An invitation to a poetry reading came with the post today and on it there were the ominous words 'wine will be served'. Why not draught Bass or Amer Picon? You give a party, you give people what they want.

As for poetry readings I prefer to read the stuff to myself and alone and vodka will be served. What the Poetry Society should be doing is giving a drink-to-me-only-with-thine-eyes party and count me out. Funny people poets. And there is another awful party which is the one where somebody walks up to you and says, 'And what do you do?' A pox on parties. Invariably there is an editor at the parties I go to who says, 'We'd love you to write a piece for us,' and then you never hear from them again. Editors of women's magazines are particularly hot at that and 'We must have lunch'. No wonder I'm so skinny.

But I have had some quite good parties sitting here at my desk by myself. After a while Great Portland Street is in soft focus which is a good thing and then I walk over to the mirror and say, 'I'm going away next week for a few days but we'll be in touch when I get back.' 'Oh, where are you going?' 'I'm going to the Coach and Horses.' 'Well, I hope the weather's good.' Now an odd thing happened after one of these solo parties recently. I had to telephone a friend and ask him, 'Is it today or is it yesterday?' The thing is the longer the days get, the more difficult it is to know whether it is morning or evening. It is as awkward as trying to find out just which town you are in without sounding completely mad. I went to a party years ago one night in Hyde Park Square and woke up in Cowes. It seemed quite a nice place just for a day and not as alarming as the time I woke up sharing a bed with a charwoman and the jockey, Barry Brogan, in a hotel in Huntingdon.

I suppose if a party is really good then it is filed away into a remote and vacant brain cell. I should have thought that they would have all been taken up with trivia by now, like what won the Derby in 1936 and that Barbara in Islington in 1951 had a green angora sweater. In fact my brain is like an old Boots Lending Library. But I have suddenly remembered who can give good parties. Racing people. The two parties Dick Hern gave on his lawn after Troy and Henbit won their Derbys were wonderful and Peter Walwyn's annual thrashes on Lurcher Show days were never to be forgotten but strangely mostly are. The gargantuan spreads attended by about 200 people he described as 'nice when a few friends pop in for a drink'.

Anyway, I am going to a racing party today in Newmarket which precedes the running of the 2,000 Guineas. The last time I went to one of Charles St George's lunch parties we never even made the racecourse and a good thing too. Newmarket may seem a long way to go for a drink but the man has style and there are some very interesting 'faces' there. They think the Prix Goncourt is a French race for two-year-olds. It makes a wonderful change from literary wine and cheese.

Driven to Drink

23 May 1987

I just heard a terrific bang and smash followed by screams, and ran out into the street to find that someone had driven a car right into the Draper's Arms. It was sitting there oozing smoke in the saloon bar. Luckily the occupants were not hurt, simply shocked. Whether they were shocked by the crash or shocked by the fact that it wasn't quite opening time is debatable. We know that a drink can often be a matter of great urgency but to actually drive into a pub is slightly over the top. (The Fire Brigade has just arrived to extract the car.) Over the years I have been kicked out of pubs, thrown out of them, forced to leave them for a lack of readies or because of the daft licensing laws but it has never taken the Fire Brigade to convince me that last orders had been called or that it was not yet opening time. (Now I have just heard that the car was parked outside the pub and that the driver – yes, yes, a woman driver – put the car into first instead of reverse.)

I think that maybe there might be a strange cosmic force, a magnetic field of sorts, something as mysterious as the Bermuda Triangle surrounding pubs. I somehow contrived a crash in the car park of the George in Lambourn once, and on another occasion, late one night, drove into the Queen's Arms in East Garston just up the road. That is one of the reasons I moved back to London where I need only the odd taxi or two a day. (The Fire Brigade has just extracted the car and an ambulance has taken the occupants away for what I hope to be a medicinal drink.) And it is still ten minutes to opening time although you wouldn't think it to look at the pub.

Yes, life – if it can be so called – in Islington is heady stuff. Why only this morning I woke up to find a spring roll in my blazer pocket. I did live in Islington once before in a house beside the canal where I used to overstay leave from my short-lived stint of National Service. That was 1950–51. The proximity of the canal made the house the only one I have ever known to be infested with frogs as opposed to mice. Such dear little things to watch hopping up the staircase.

But it is alleged that there was once another strange incident involving the Fire Brigade and a pub. It took place some years ago in the Queen's Elm in the Fulham Road. A nutter called Eileen, known to all as The Fox, one day dialled 999 and asked for the Fire Brigade. They arrived with sirens screaming, leaped from the engine hoses in hand and asked, 'Where's the fire?' The Fox lifted up her skirt and said 'In here, boys.' I think she got three months. What she should have got was nine. (The builders have arrived already and they are clearing up the mess. We should be on target for the one in twenty minutes.)

But a good man to have next to you when there's a fire is Peter Langan who extinguishes the awful things with champagne. (Peter died horribly in a fire subsequently, but he was a man who was readily amused by disasters. He may be laughing now.) And I have just remembered something. And don't stop me if I've told you but the house with the frogs in Islington was owned by a woman who had a grocer's shop. She didn't live there but she kept, God knows why, a drum of maple syrup in the hall on the ground floor. One day it fell over. Now, it has probably never crossed your mind and why should it but it is a strange experience to come home late at night after having taken refreshment to find yourself rooted to the spot in a sea of syrup. One survived. Others didn't. With Newton it was apples. With frogs it was syrup. I suppose one should have cooked the legs of the poor blighters. (The 'Business as Usual' sign has just gone up.)

Which reminds me, the firemen from the fire station in Shaftesbury Avenue drink in the Coach and Horses and what a fit, strong and brave bunch of lads they are. Can you imagine scaling one of those ladders to enter an inferno to rescue someone? They probably don't get paid very much either. One of them told me that one person a day in Great Britain dies through falling asleep drunk with a cigarette. Perhaps that is why the Government say they can seriously damage your health. Anyway, I am now going to telephone the Fire Brigade to see if they can get me *into* the pub. Through the roof if necessary.

Meanwhile I shall be 55 on Thursday. No flowers please. Fifty-five. That's just about enough. Much more would be a kind of greed, but maybe just the gloomy one more.

Egyptian Daddy

30 May 1987

I keep thinking of the nutty reader who wrote to me and said, 'What a wonderful life you must lead.' Well I suppose it is by a tramp's standards but I am beginning to wonder just when I shall run out of friends willing to put me up while the search for a flat goes on and on and on. Finding the source of the Nile was a doddle compared to this game. And I am beginning to get up very late in the morning which is a bad sign but what is there to get up *for*? Other signs of giving way are dirty fingernails, wearing a shirt for two consecutive days and not bothering to shave. I tell you it's midway through Waterloo and I can't for the life of me see Blucher on the horizon.

But having said all that I must say that Islington grows on me. The architecture I mentioned a couple of weeks ago plus the trees and the gardens are very comforting. I wish I had been old enough to appreciate Holland Park while I was growing up there during the war. My mother could have bought our lovely house for peanuts then but peanuts were never the strong suit of this family.

But here's an odd thing. The gloom and monotony of low life was broken this week by an extraordinary telephone call I received in the pub. A woman aged 38 called to inform me that I am her father. She came into the pub five years ago to give me the same story but I then thought I would never hear from her again. Now she has cropped up again. I did in fact lose my virginity – why *lose*? I gave it away gladly – to her mother when I was 15 years old in 1947, so I could theoretically be her father, but I am damned sure I am not. She said that someone has just lent her a copy of my book and that she can tell from the photograph taken of me when I was young that I am definitely dad. She said that at the same age our eyebrows were exactly the same. Dark brown and hairy. I can't see that standing up in court, not that she wants anything from me, but eyebrows? I ask you.

What she probably wants – she was adopted – is a father and I can guess just how she feels. I would like a father too. I am up to here with mothers and I wouldn't hazard a guess at how many of them I have had over the past 30 years. But I suspect that she just wants to belong. Well, she's welcome for what it's worth. She then went on to say that having read *Low Life* she thinks I am very sensitive. Now that was nice. Up till now I thought I was simply soft in the head. But it is a little odd at the age of 38 to still crave a father, or is it?

I would like my daughter, I know, but I don't see much of her. But next month I hope to take her on a cruise up the Nile. At least that will be something she will *never* forget. Who knows, I might even find an unfurnished flat in Luxor. Anyway, she is thrilled by the idea, but what does a 17-year-old girl do while her father is stretched out pissed in a deckchair getting sunstroke and throwing ice-cubes at the crocodiles? Her mother says there will be lots of people for her to talk to. Lots of people? What sort? I can't imagine anyone less wonderful than Graham Greene and Eric Ambler characters on a Nile steamer but I know in my heart that they will in reality be a dull bunch of tourists. Aren't we all?

I don't think I am exactly dull but I do dread the glazed-eyed boredom that comes over the faces of barmen and waiters in foreign lands when I approach. But then, of course, most people dislike each other. Until they get to know each other and then it can be loathing. But talking of the daughter, Isabel, I was extremely shocked – and I mean it – to hear the other day that her mother found an empty bottle of Chablis in her room. Homework? A half-bottle yes. An empty whole bottle, no. I hope it was a good one though and not the sort of crap they sell in Wheeler's. I thought these people had pop music and discos to stop them from thinking, but it would seem not.

What next? Yes, of course. An affair with an Egyptian cabin boy. I think I might creep quietly into a pyramid and lay me down to die. I am mummified already anyway. And now, daddified.

Kippers are Off

13 June 1987

I should have been with you last week but I was as sick as a dog. The pancreas is infuriated again. How anyone can eat sweetbreads is beyond me. It was too depressing to linger alone in bed in the Islington basement so I moved in with a very kind friend nearby for a couple of days and then, when I felt I was becoming a nuisance to her, I moved into a hotel in Frith Street to try and recover and lick the wounds. I can tell you that the hotel lark in London is a bloody expensive business, but I thought that room service might be a nurse of sorts that I didn't have to be beholden to. Room service is a Spanish woman out of Fawlty Towers who had to be taught how to make tea properly. She was making a pot of the stuff with only one tea-bag and whatever happened to loose tea?

Anyway, I have been lying here staring at the ceiling and having many morbid thoughts about Oscar Wilde dying in a hotel room. Not that it matters much where you die as long as it doesn't inconvenience friends, but it would be nicer to exit stage left to a round of applause than to be discovered by room service who scream fearfully on such occasions in all the Hollywood movies I have ever seen. Poor Oscar. Of course, the only thing that would make the French room service scream would be the thought of the deceased not having paid his or her bill. But this is a nice enough hotel done up in a mock Victorian style with reproduction brass fittings on the bath and room furniture that doesn't stink of the age of Utility and the 1940s. Unfortunately the walls and the ceiling I stare at are paper thin and the noise reminds me of being in hospital where the nurses will do anything for you except allow you to sleep at night.

On the second morning here I decided I couldn't face another pot of weak tea and a croissant for £3.50 so I staggered out to try to find a proper breakfast and the sad thing is that the traditional workman's café has all but disappeared. It is very sad. London is now littered with the most awful sandwich bars. Whatever happened to eggs, bacon, sausages, tomatoes and bubble and squeak? Sandwiches wrapped in clingfilm and take-away cardboard cups of instant coffee are another sign of these awful times we live in. But in some ways they are preferable to the alternative cults of lunatics like Jane Fonda and her ilk. I would also like to know why it is that you can't get a *boiled* egg anywhere. And another thing: you can't get a kipper in the café – if you can find a café – because the owners say a kipper stinks all day. They don't smell all day in the Savoy or the Ritz, though, I've noticed.

Anyway, it is pointless to chew the cud over such matters and it is like reminiscing about dead friends. So, on the way back from the fruitless search for a simple breakfast I tottered into the Coach for a cup of coffee and some Perrier water. Our host took me to one side to express the opinion that apart from my pancreas he thought that having no fixed abode was killing me. The man is a sleuth.

But even though I am tapping for coda, as musicians say about someone on the brink, I can't help feeling slightly amused by the looks people have given me since I have been ill. I have seen those expressions so many times on the faces of visitors sitting around the bedsides of the doomed when I have been in hospitals. It is a look of concern badly veneered with jollity. In hospitals this look is accompanied by such catchphrases as, 'You'll be up in no time.' 'You're looking much better today.' When you come out . . . ' 'The doctor says you're coming along fine.' Etc. etc. And sometimes you can see the captive audience lying in his bed thinking, 'Why don't you piss off and leave me in peace?'

Anyway, I am determined to be back on my feet to take the daughter up the Nile next month. I would hate to go up it *à la* Dr Livingstone's last trip, on a stretcher. That would be impossible anyway nowadays since it is very unlikely that one could find four porters willing to do the job. It must have been terribly depressing for Livingstone to have been found by a hack in the jungle. It is unthinkable that a man busy exploring something or other and wishing to be left in peace in his swamp or jungle should come face to face with a *Guardian* hack.

Absent Friends

27 June 1987

The speed at which friends are being flung out into the void seems to be accelerating. If I believed in life after death I would say that there must be a hell of a party going on somewhere out there. And there's room for more. This week it was the turn of Dennis 'Pip' Piper who was a dear chap and a friend since 1949. He was a designer of great gift and until recently he was art director of the *Economist*. He was also, for the last 15 years or so of his life, a non-drinking alcoholic which was a condition he coped with quite admirably. He wasn't a poacher turned gamekeeper as such people so often are, he was simply a retired poacher without any traces of self-righteousness or evangelical ambitions which are common among sometime members of AA.

He wasn't a withdrawn and miserable teetotaller and his rate for buying a round of drinks never decreased. Abstinence suited him and when his cancer was diagnosed he didn't find it necessary to go back to the first and last resort of the anxious and frightened. I can hear his lisp now and the way he prefixed his sentences by saying, 'Lithen man . . . ' Five of us once went to a ridiculous amount of trouble to manoeuvre him into Wheelers so that we could hear him order the first course. It came out as, 'We'd like thixth muthel thoupth pleath.' He then immediately tumbled our childish design, turned to us and said, 'You bathtardth.' But he was amused, which was more than I was by the awful advice he gave me just before I went up for my medical for National Service. Having been an armoured car (Dingo) driver himself he said to put down for a tank regiment, the theory being that I wouldn't have to go on any route marches. How wrong he was. For years until now it made for wry smiles of recrimination from me and guffaws from him.

During the 1960s we ate hundreds of lunches in the Trattoria Terrazza together with other ghosts like Frank Norman. That was when the drink really got to him. He ate less and less and he used to actually *pick* at a quail, leave half of it and wash that small amount down with vast quantities of Calvados. Then he cracked and the medical profession didn't help him a lot by overprescribing tranquillizers and electric shock treatment. It says a lot for his fortitude and *sense* that he survived to be as unscrewed up as he was. He never had another drink. But he had his jazz. An enormous collection of it and an encyclopaedic knowledge of it. He bought jazz records like other people buy newspapers. He told a mutual friend not long ago that when he died he would rather be mentioned in this column than be the subject of a *Times* obituary. I wish it was a pleasure to oblige.

Pip brings the total number of deaths of friends over the last five years to an unacceptable amount. To an outsider one may seem to be very matter-of-fact about it, but that isn't so. It is just that the death of friends is no longer *surprising*. After 50 not much is. Thirty years ago, when John Minton committed suicide, it should have been obvious that he was the thin end of the wedge of death that we've all been nibbling at. I used to think about him a lot and also my first wife, Anna, who killed herself too. Now months go by without a thought for them or a glance into the driving mirror, so to speak. Now, Pip's death sadly revives memories of all of them who are not to appear in today's matinée. Elizabeth Smart, Jeremy Madden-Simpson, Eva, and Peter Dunbar, Pip's predecessor at the *Economist* have gone recently. It is a crazy play and the understudies are understandably reluctant to go on.

And just for once I shall not go to a friend's funeral. I am sick of the cautious and embarrassed looks the survivors give each other and there is nothing much to say anyway. People don't want to be made to feel guilty about being alive and it may be coming to that. For once I feel grateful for being lower down in the batting order than I thought I was. I was going to spend a weekend in the country with Pip the other day and opted out of it. That would have been good just as his company always was. It is all of it a crying shame.

Baby Talk

4 July 1987

Whatever happened to herpes? Now that AIDS is with us it barely gets a look-in. I don't feel as sorry for it as I would for a man whose obituary was spiked in favour of a bigger name on the day, but you hardly hear the word on anyone's lips these days. It is just that it occurs to me that you can date people and slot them into their generation if you know about their venereal past record, dreads and expectancies. When I was a lad, the boys dreaded clap and the girls were terrified of getting pregnant. Now, I am not frightened of catching anything – the chance might be a fine thing – and I haven't seen an obviously pregnant woman for years. You used to see them everywhere dragging their weary feet in and out of shops but the first evidence you see of it nowadays is your actual baby itself.

I don't like babies very much. They haven't got a lot to say and their mothers will keep using them as battering rams in supermarkets. Oddly enough they are quite sensitive to atmosphere and I made one cry yesterday by giving it a dirty look. Its nose was running, it was sucking a comforter and was dressed up as a rabbit. Comforters, dummies or whatever you may like to call them, look particularly disgusting on middle-aged and elderly babies. If I had the misfortune to become a father again I would shove a cigarette into baby's mouth should it start howling because of a surfeit of dirty looks.

The present daughter didn't cry much when she was a baby and I can only assume she was too daft to realize her home was breaking up and that she was having an unhappy childhood. I think she cries a bit now after her driving lessons, but she is at present beaming at the thought of steaming up the Nile with me. Last night I took her to a pub and allowed her to play with the traveller's cheques while she sipped a Pernod. Then, over a rather expensive dinner, she complained that the Pernod had spoiled the taste of the wine. It is not a good idea to spoil a daughter because of guilt feelings about ten years ago, but what else can you do? But I think that if I hadn't seen my father from the age of two until 17 and then he walked in somewhere I was and asked, 'Same again?' I would be quite pleased.

Anyway, the dreaded Isabel looked over my shoulder a few minutes ago and said, 'Oh, you're writing about AIDS. It's my favourite subject.' 'At school?' I asked, quite astonished. 'No. On television.' She has had an appalling education and I am a little sceptical about teachers wanting more money. Well, not so much *wanting* more, but being able to justify more. It could be that I breathed too many Teacher's over Isabel once and she shut off. She is opening up now though and this morning I heard her come in at 4.30 a.m. She even got up before midday thanks to a telephone call from her mother – the wife I thought was Captain Oates when she left me but who made a remarkable recovery to come in from the cold – and she is at the moment watching an a.m. showing of *Dallas* in spite of the fact that I have just advised her that the pubs are now open.

Which reminds me of another awful thing about schools today. Kids seem to know nothing about the history of their own wretched country. Isabel thinks that the Duke of Wellington is a pub. Well, it is, but would I have about 15 biographies of a pub plus a volume of the landlord's despatches from the Peninsular coach outing? I think the intense heat in Egypt might snap her out of this rather vague thinking. I see from the *Times* that it was 95°F in Cairo yesterday which means it is probably about 100°F between Luxor and Aswan. I can't wait to play the John Clements part in *The Four Feathers*. When I told Isabel about it her eyes glazed over slightly and I suspect she thinks that the mad Mahdi and General Gordon were a pop group and a pub respectively.

But where oh where is contentment? I shall be worried out of my mind about the Headingley Test Match and I shall miss the Coral Eclipse Stakes at Sandown Park on Saturday. And now Isabel has just announced that she wants to climb up a pyramid from the inside. The idea of such horrifying claustrophobia makes me feel sick and does, I think, justify just the one and first of the day.

Pharaoh-noia

18 July 1987

To stand hatless in the Valley of the Kings in a temperature of 115°F while afflicted with very serious diarrhoea is faintly ridiculous and rather frightening. You daren't move. I stood there staring at the mountains wondering what does it all mean and that is a subject only fit for contemplation when alone in bed at night. The sun was drilling my skull for blood. There was some sand in my mouth and the colonic spasms made me drip sweat. *That* is what I remember most vividly of Egypt. That and the river Nile itself. Temples, tombs and ruins are strictly for tourists gazing in groups and I prefer to be alone and find my own sights.

I never meant to get sucked into a group and it was foolish of me to imagine I wouldn't be when we set sail from Aswan to go downstream to Luxor. Groups hellbent on 'sightseeing' shuffle along in a slow-moving queue avaricious for anything of antiquity and quick on the draw with a camera. And I wonder how well Kodak do out of the film wasted on the other obsession of the tourist – the *views*. You really need something a little special other than a Pentax to take pictures of views and local postcards are best. But the group from the boat seemed to think I was an oddball sloping off to find my own views which didn't register with any of them. In a refreshment bar near King Tutankhamun's tomb, where I found a lavatory with as much wonder as Carter experienced in 1922 on opening that tomb, I watched dried-up old Arabs smoking their pipes and drinking coffee over endless games of backgammon. I drank very cold beer and liked it for the first time in years.

When the group came in at last after having seen the tombs of generations of kings they immediately got into line for Coca-Colas and 7-Ups and they seemed to look disturbed at my drinking beer. After all, wasn't I just about the only person of about 300 on the boat who drank alcohol in the lounge bar? It was the same sort of hostility tempered with curiosity that I felt steaming up the Mississippi from New Orleans to Memphis and cruising around the fjords of Norway between Oslo and the North Cape. On the Nile it occurred to me that if travel broadens the mind then Australians and Americans set out with precious little of it.

But there was a strange atmosphere in both the Valley of the Kings and the Valley of the Queens. Perhaps I am romancing or letting my imagination run away with me but the feeling of time and an age going back 4,000 years made me feel as though I was being watched. The desert and the mountains had, after all, soaked up so many people over the years and the old Egyptian preoccupation with death and the dead somehow lingered in those scorched and blistered rocks and sand. Fanciful maybe, but that is how it was to me. On the way back to the banks of the Nile where a ramshackle ferry waited to take us back to our luxury boat our coach stopped to allow the group to photograph an old pillar and to buy some papyrus. Watching people barter bores me. Trying to do it myself embarrasses me but it seems to be obligatory. They actually like being knocked down, these street traders. We had stopped on a muddy lane in the fertile sugar-cane fields that accompany the river from Aswan to Luxor. The camera buffs didn't see the dog lying in a puddle and panting from the heat or the open-doored tin sheds with old women inside seated at tables and emulating the miracle of the loaves and the fishes. A small boy drove a flock of goats with expertise but the Canons and Nikons, aimed at the old pillar, chattered away like castanets.

Back on the boat I witnessed the largest order for Coca-Cola the world has ever known. Into mine I poured some vodka out of my duty-free bottle, and was spotted doing so by an Australian teacher in charge of a revolting crocodile – the only one on the Nile – of 26 schoolgirls. She turned to her companion, an overweight PE teacher, and said, 'That isn't allowed. Should we report him?' A combination of heat and impatience with middle-class Australian priggishness prompted me to lean forward and suggest she mind her own f———ing business.

I had hoped to meet the lovable Sir Les Patterson or some of the wonderful drunken wits who jeer at the English from the Hill at Sydney cricket ground but no such luck. But I did make one little friend on the boat – an American 14-year-old boy called Phillip who is an amalgam of Huckleberry Finn and Portnoy. He deserves to be laid very soon by a discerning and sympathetic woman. When we disembarked at Luxor to fly back to Cairo my bar bill was £E102. His was £E80. His father was not pleased but being a professor of genetics probably managed to rationalize it. My daughter Isabel's bar bill was £E32 for four days' Coca-Cola which struck me as being fairly revolting. I don't think she liked the holiday much and she is not yet sufficiently streetwise not to be intimidated by waiters, hotel porters and taxi drivers. Anyway, for her, anyone over 21 is geriatric, although she told me she made some 'pen friends' from the group of Australian schoolgirls. It remains to be seen whether anyone can actually write. At least Isabel has learned the wonder of signing bar bills.

On our last day we went to see the pyramids and the Sphinx and took pictures of each other standing in front of them. An Arab insisted on taking a picture of me holding on to his camel. Disgusting animals. All the while our own personal guide spouted history lessons. All I wanted to know was how Egyptians live *today*. After all, can they have so much regard for archaeology who kept Egyptian railways running for a ten-year period using no other fuel than mummies? But I shall remember the Nile especially during its brief sunsets. The heat of the day makes the sky white and not blue and when the sun does go down over those angry orange carbuncles of mountains, it is also pale and yellow. Then the colour of the river changes too and it becomes as gunmetal. The distant chanting of calls to prayer are only interrupted by calls for Coca-Cola on the boat. I hope the ghosts of the old kings get angry one day.

Writer's Block

25 July 1987

This week has been rotten so far and it is only Tuesday today from where I am sitting. Yesterday, I saw Anthony Burgess in Old Compton Street, called out to him, but he pressed on. I found that strangely depressing and then bumped into Jay Landesman who didn't press on and that was depressing too. And, at the moment, it is raining, probably will for ever, and I am due to picnic at the Oval tomorrow, go to Cherbourg the day after and finally picnic again at Ascot for the King George VI and Queen Elizabeth Diamond Stakes.

I am also living with two cats, one of which, called Alice, is really rather awful. Can you imagine a cat being so fat that you can actually *hear* it walk across a carpet? Also, the said cat does not sit on the mat. It sleeps on my temporary litter. Alice's friend and enemy, Stanley, is out all night and sleeps in the kitchen all day which is just what you expect of a self-respecting tom. But I don't like Alice and I don't want whatever lives in her tabby fur coat in my bed. She doesn't like me either and thinks that I have evicted her holiday-making owners from their house. Anyway, that's what it has come down to. Cat-sitting in return for a bed, and being snubbed by Anthony Burgess. I felt so gloomy that I went to the Groucho Club and complained at them for not doing cucumber sandwiches on a summer's afternoon.

They are so good to me there that I feel rotten about that now. Cucumbers are for Pimms. Another disturbing thing, speaking of the Groucho, is that strange women in there keep nodding to me and mouthing good afternoons. I don't know them. What on earth have I said or done or not done? To cap it all I was interviewed by a woman from *Balance*, the magazine of the British Diabetic Association. Why their readers should want to read about how I break the rules heaven alone knows, but diabetics, I have noticed, don't half go on about it. Then a man from another magazine came into the pub to photograph me. This sort of thing must be done in private in future if there is any future. It upsets thespian friends so much to see anybody else get paid some attention let alone get served in the Coach and Horses.

Thank God for the fact that so few of Norman's customers are members of the Groucho. Should that last bolthole become a sort of Milton Keynes for the insane I should have to go and live abroad. I shall have to go and live somewhere in ten days' time anyway. Alice and Stanley's owners return. If any reader needs a cat-sitter who has given up smoking in bed then please let me know. I will sit for dogs but will not walk them or guide them through the revolving doors of the Groucho Club. Yes, it's wet and cold and I suppose if I had been walking along Old Compton Street a hundred-odd years ago Charles Dickens would have snubbed me. Two years ago, Burgess once spent an afternoon in the Colony Room Club telling me the meaning of life. The trouble is I have forgotten what he said which is why I tried to buttonhole him yesterday.

Jay Landesman knows the meaning of life but unfortunately, being American, he can't speak English. I was sent his autobiography recently to review, but how can you give a bad review to an old friend and ex-publisher? Tricky one, that. I suppose you can lie or write it under a pseudonym. Perhaps the thing would be to say to Jay, 'You should have written it yourself Who needs ghosts?' The truth is I am envious of all the publicity he has had. Also the fact that he has a house and is married to a very clever woman. I have had both of those luxuries but am now about to move into a single tent in the camping department of Lillywhites.

It was a wise man – probably Anthony Burgess – who once said that it never rains but it pours and looking out of the window I see that it is doing just that. A taxi to Soho seems to be in order and I shall leave a tin opener for Alice to work it out for herself.

Vaguely Sinister

5 September 1987

For the past three days I have been sharing a breakfast table with no less than seven women. Extraordinary things women. I find them quite fascinating. They haven't had a conversation in three hours. Oh, they talk all right, but it is all fragmented trivia. From what time we went to bed last night to I think I'll pour myself another cup of tea. Pour the bloody tea, madam, and don't feel obliged to announce your intention of doing so. And they sit very precisely, yet within three minutes a plate of two eggs, bacon, sausage and tomatoes plus a rack of toast has vanished. There's something vaguely sinister about that. The ones that paint talk about money and the ones who don't need to do anything talk about 'art'.

They are very wary of me – my miserable face I suppose – and their 'Good mornings' are hushed. It is terrible to be unintentionally forbidding. I want them to pour out their little thumping hearts to me. Bless them.

It was even worse in Soho on Bank Holiday Monday. I had

to go there to cash a cheque. I only stayed an hour, but it was painful. Communication is via anecdote in the British pub. Apparently Jim got drunk on Sunday. Conan was in on Saturday evening, Michael was over the moon because Arsenal won 6–0 and Jill had an Indian take-away on Friday – no, I tell a lie, was it the Thursday? Yes, it was Thursday. Oh, and Tino got mugged in the Elephant and Castle on the way home on the Saturday, or was it the Friday? No, it was the Sunday, because Susie and Paul were in here.

It was bliss to get back to the garden where I am staying, although one man had to tell me that it is a funny old life. I spend quite a lot of time being fed bits of information like that, which is just as well when you consider that an idle mind is the playground of the devil.

Now, apart from the reluctance, inability or disinterest of so many people when it comes to discussing the human condition, I notice that many people are becoming deranged with visual forms of comunication. As I write to you, at this very minute an American woman is snapping her camera at the man who is mowing the lawn. But what American tourists really go in for is filming *static* objects with cine cameras. Things like the Admiralty Arch or St Paul's Cathedral. (St Paul's is sliding down the hill, I am told, at a rate of one eighth of an inch a year.) Yesterday I watched a Japanese man filming his wife getting out of a taxi. He needed three takes for satisfaction. I really don't see the need to record that one little thread of the vast tapestry of his wife's life.

I don't have a photograph of my first wife, but I do of the next three and no taxies are involved. One of them left me in *my* car, one of them left me in a pub and another in a huff. You would be surprised how long a huff can last. It is not to be confused with a puff. But I aimed the camera at all three of them while they were still smiling and before the dawn of their dreadful realizations of their mistake. It is strange to see how growing disappointment can change a woman's face. No, it isn't strange: it is bloody awful.

The American lady is now photographing a brick wall. It could be 'art'. I knew a man who spent a lot of his time photographing rocks.

Another art form is the cooking of my friend Graham Mason's common-law wife. He was sipping some consommé that she had made for him on the Bank Holiday Monday and two of his front teeth fell out. Is this taking *al dente* cooking too far? He can no longer smile without embarrassment. On the other hand, he has not got much to smile about.

Publicans' Holiday *19 September 1987*

There's a splendid woman who is the landlady of a good pub in Islington and who always has something a little odd to tell me when I drop in to see her. Last night she told me that she had recently been on a trip to Florida with 200 publicans. I can't think of anything more awful at the moment. Pass the bottle. Yes, they took over an aeroplane for themselves. They told the airline to stock up with plenty of extra booze, which they did, and in spite of that the aircraft was dry one and a half hours before it landed at Miami. Then they all stayed in the same hotel. Shambles, wouldn't you think? Here we go, here we go, here we go.

But what was remarkable was that they went sea fishing one day and her old dad, a retired publican, hooked a blue marlin twice his own size. He is blind. What an incredible sensation it must have been for him to fight against an unseen strength like that. Take a blind ex-publican from Chapel Street Market, well into his sixties, push him out into the Atlantic and you have the real old man and the sea. They asked the old man if he would like the marlin to be stuffed so that he could take it home with him but he said no, he didn't want to pay the excess baggage money. What annoys him most about being blind, it seems, is that he can no longer read the form. His wife, poor thing, has to read it out to him every morning and not long ago he won just over £1,000 with a mere 50p yankee. If he fell down a drain he'd come up holding a fiver.

Anyway, as soon as they got back to London the landlady, Janet, had to throw a wedding party upstairs in the pub. She told me that it went on until 3.30 a.m. I asked her if there was any trouble. (You understand that her customers, though domiciled in Islington, do not read the *Guardian*.) She said, 'Oh no, my customers are all very *kind*.' My italics. Then she went on to say, 'Funny thing, though. My mum went to a party at the Savoy last month and there was a terrible punch-up.' Well, some of them can throw punches as well as bread rolls, I told her. Then she bought me a drink as she always does. She just takes your glass away and tops it up without saying a word. How I wish that pub and she could be transported to Soho Square.

Then, the next day, I bumped into another face from Islington, dear old Charlie who once had a stall in Berwick Street market. He is very much missed in Soho by some of us. Me anyway. He gave me a tremendous hug, something I don't want from many people, but it was oddly very moving. He isn't embarrassed to show affection. What a strange man he is. He has had only sufficient education to enable him to write out a betting slip, he is an ex-con and tearaway, and yet he has a pretty profound knowledge of and insight into the human condition. On the other hand he was daft enough, when I first met him, to think I was an intellectual because I own a tripewriter. We used to creep off to the Piccadilly Hotel to drink when we got bored with Soho and he'd give me what he considered to be a playful punch in the ribs and say, 'So how's all your intellectual friends then, Jeffrey?'

That was only three years ago and he had an awful mistress then. He used to take her to a hotel in Bloomsbury most afternoons, which cost him £35. He also always took a bottle of champagne with him, plus a present for her and a bag of his rather dubious fruit. An expensive hobby, and when you think of the amount of vodka he drank before the bubbly a miracle of medical science too. I must be getting too sentimental in my old age but when I think of the greeting he gave me I feel very touched. Friends are more valuable even than books. I suppose the awful thing about sentimentality is that it stems from self-pity. Even Hitler liked dogs and children. How very English of him.

Travels With Myself

10 October 1987

The Lord giveth all right but he doesn't half take it away again. Last Sunday at Longchamp, drinking Victor Chandler's champagne and Rocco Forte's vodka, I forgot for the length of time that it took Trempolino to cover the distance of the Arc that I still have nowhere to live and have therefore run out of jokes.

Other people haven't run out of jokes though. I bumped into one punter in Paris who said to me, 'Why don't you move into the Coach and Horses?' I thought that was so excruciatingly funny, I had to pour a glass of red wine over him for fear his wit would damage my ribs. I sometimes wish I was still capable of hitting some people.

Apart from the nasty nocturne in St Germain it was a splendid weekend. Victor and Rocco's hospitality was the icing on the top of a good cake. I only had one bet, Polonia, and she cruised up at 7–1. The friend I stayed with who works for the *Herald Tribune* was delightful, the food was memorable, and the weather was gorgeous. Eating lunch and even dinner outside in the sunshine and under the stars at the Brasserie St Benoit made the Middlesex Hospital, the Inland Revenue, the Booker Prize, Mrs Thatcher, the litter of London and my bar bill at the Groucho Club seem a million miles away. But the trouble with travel is that it doesn't remove you from yourself. When Marco Polo finally got to China he was probably worrying that he hadn't locked the kitchen door behind him.

On the first night in Paris, I bumped into an old friend who now lives there. He was legless. Not an amputee, as one American understood the expression to mean, just drunk as a rat. We passed a jolly hour in a bar and then the next day I bumped into his wife. She said, quite severely, 'So you got my old man drunk last night.' That annoyed me nearly as much as the punter who suggested I live in the pub. Why, oh why, do women think their husbands are always led astray by their friends? It is ridiculous and bloody rude and you wouldn't exactly have to put an arm lock on this particular friend to get a bottle of whisky down him.

The next time I go to Paris I shall keep myself to myself, apart from having the one with some of the people who work on the *Herald Tribune*. They drink in a bar called the Village and the odd thing is that it is the twin bar to the Coach and Horses. The only difference really is that you can get served in the Village.

And now I am preparing for another journey next month to Kenya, hopefully. I have had a kind invitation from a reader of this column to go and stay at Karen Blixen's old place while she and her husband go elsewhere on holiday. I must say that it's a rather stylish way of solving the bed and breakfast situation for two or three weeks. In a letter outlining the dos and don'ts of Kenya, she advises me that I don't need anti-malaria pills unless I intend to go on safari. I have had some very weird fantasies in my time but my imagination could never stomach the thought of going on safari. This column is not signed Hemingway.

The other thing that caught my eye in her letter is the fact that there are no dangerous animals about, although a leopard did make off with their dog. So a leopard isn't dangerous? And how should it know the difference between me and a dog? I look like an anorexic whippet.

But I love the idea of going to Africa. John Hurt has nearly finished building a house nearby and perhaps we will be able to lead each other astray, difficult as that may be. And will the natives be restless, I wonder? I can't stop thinking about safaris now. I really don't see me with a pith helmet and shorts. I'd as soon walk down Oxford Street in pyjamas if I had any.

The Harder They Fall

31 October 1987

It is all so horribly sad. Yes, I know he was guilty, but that is neither here nor there as far as my feelings are concerned. The ruin of a national hero is not to be gloated over and if you say that Lester Piggott got what he deserved then you are missing my point. You might also be a little self-righteous, although you would be right to be appalled at greed on such a mammoth scale. What I don't like is the fact that until Lester was arrested his legendary avarice and much exaggerated meanness were one of racing's favourite jokes and a source of endless funny anecdotes. But now he is a man who 'got what he deserved'. Last Saturday morning I woke up and realized that he was slopping out and then being given a mug of tea and a slice of bread and margarine. What a very depressing picture and how very odd that at this moment of writing my brother Oliver is hell bent on joining him in HM Prison Norwich for his CND activities.

Apart from being so greedy Lester has been remarkably *silly*. He has always been too secretive to ask anyone with knowledge of things beyond racing for advice. Newmarket may not be a one-horse town but it is a one-solicitor town, so to speak. He should have made friends with people like Lord Goodman as soon as he passed the post on Never Say Die in 1954. He should have seen it coming or somebody should have told him.

The last time I spoke to Lester was outside the weighing room at Epsom on Derby Day. He treated me to a couple of his rare smiles but you could see that he had faced up to the fact that he was going to go down. The time before that was at Chantilly where we had a rather strange encounter in the jockey's changing room. I had gone over there for *Tatler* who had lumbered me with a rather daft female paparazzo. Lester had just had a shower and we were chatting away, he stark naked, and the girl standing in the doorway at the other end of the room didn't even have the wit to take a picture.

But to go back to people's strange reactions to the verdict last week. BBC's *Newsnight* brought a crew to the Coach and Horses to interview me about the matter. I waffled to them for a while in the upstairs room and they then went down to the bar to get a comment or two from the customers in the bar plus Norman who thinks the Derby is run at Wembley. With a smug smile on his face and with his well-considered wisdom he said, 'In view of the seriousness of the offence, I think he got what he deserved.' They moved on to a man, slightly the worse for wear, who said, 'They should have given him a knighthood.' But then they questioned a ghastly scrubber who snarled, 'He should have got ten years.' What amazing vindictiveness coming from a girl who should have been serving ten years herself for the hat she was wearing.

Now I am wondering how they will treat Lester in the nick. In about four weeks' time he will most likely be moved to an open prison and I suppose he will be an object of great curiosity for a while, as he has been to me since that Derby in 1954. I can't imagine what work they will put him to. Keeper of the prison governor's cigars might suit, but I can't see him working in the library unless they have a subscription to *Timeform*. Oh hell, I shall really miss him. Can you imagine London without Nelson's column? Boiled eggs without salt? Lester Piggott was always essential and many of us feel bereaved.

By now it is midday and brother Oliver may be on his way to Norwich prison. What an extraordinary encounter that might be. It would be like locking up Keats with Jack Dempsey. What would they talk about? The food most likely.

Bwana in Suburbia

14 November 1987

Nairobi

This is very different to anything I have known before. I have never felt so abroad before. Moscow, Luxor and New Orleans might well have been at the end of the Piccadilly Line, but Africa feels like something else, a sort of mystical dream. I wake up and feel as though I am in Islington, draw the curtains and it is Africa. And I have only been here three days.

Karen is a suburb of Nairobi, a city that James Cameron once referred to as 'equatorial Ealing'. Karen itself is not too bad and the house I am staying in could be almost anywhere between Haslemere and Sunningdale. Very British indeed. It is a solid, stone-built house with parquet floors, some wood-panelled walls, lattice windows and ingle-nooks. There is a lovely garden and you would call this place a desirable residence if you were an estate agent.

At dawn the bird song is staccato, an octave above a blackbird, and the flowers in the garden don't match. Orange, mauve and magenta beneath grey-green flat-topped trees are the colours of a nouveau riche racehorse owner. There are sun-birds everywhere, doves coo, a hawk perches on a dead branch miles high, and when the early morning rain subsides there comes a stillness as though nature itself were a frozen frame taken from a movie.

I haven't slept well, and in the early hours I can hear the two guards murmuring to each other outside the front door. Break-ins are very common and insurance companies insist on guards and iron gates over every window and door. Before I came here I got hooked on the idea of Kenya mainly through reading James Fox's *White Mischief*, and since being here I have read Elspeth Huxley and John Hillaby, both in one sitting, and I can't stop reading more and more about this amazing country. I lie there drinking pint after pint of tea, waiting for the dawn and light.

At 8 a.m. Joyce arrives to feed the dogs and cats and to make more tea. She always surprises me since she wears no shoes and so makes not a sound until she says, 'Would sir like some more tea?' She is a *Guardian* women's page reader's nightmare. I only have to look at anything at all and she immediately washes it and then irons it. She would probably iron the lawn if the gardener fell ill. On Sunday she surprised me by turning up to feed the animals, empty my ashtray and fill my ice-bucket wearing a spotless white Salvation Army uniform. It looked very good on her, her skin being so black as to be almost navy blue.

Then I have a driver, John, an ex-police driver who is as impassive as granite. I can't quite get used to his willingness to wait for me outside supermarkets and hotels. I feel uncomfortable. Servants we had when I was five years old, but at that age they were family and friends: nannies, temperamental cooks and alcoholic gardeners. God knows where my father found them.

This evening I sat just inside the open french windows and watched a deluge. Behind me there was a crackling log fire and who could ask for a better companion? But the rain wasn't a sad inconvenience like English rain. It was a symptom of a life force like a storm at sea.

But back to the people and the Englishness of it all. I had lunch in the Aero Club yesterday at Wilson Airport with a local pilot who offered me a lift to Malindi and a white hunter. The w.h. wasn't very Hemingway but he looked very strong and had such pale blue eyes I could see them staring down the sights of a high-velocity rifle. In passing, I said that I wasn't particularly frightened of snakes. He looked at my jodhpur boots and said, 'A puff adder could bite right through one of those.' So far I have only met a spider in the pantry and a large black mouse. And so I have now invited an aggressive cat to share my bed.

But there are worse things than dangerous animals in Kenya. I read to my horror yesterday that a tribe from Ethiopia raid north-western Kenya and are required to return home with as many testicles as they can possibly remove to prove their manhood. Presumably their wives have airmail subscriptions to the *Guardian* too.

The End of the Line

5 December 1987

Kisumu

I am sitting here in Kisumu on the shores of Lake Victoria in a patio bar under the shade of a bamboo roof. I arrived by train from Nairobi early this morning and have now travelled the length of this extraordinary and one-time slightly mad railway from Mombasa to Kisumu.

From Nairobi the train ascends to Nikuru through the most fertile land I have ever seen outside the east of Lebanon, the valley on the border with Syria, the legendary site of the Garden of Eden. The train climbs up to Nikuru through red earth scattered with maize, vegetables and banana plants. As it gets higher the earth turns brown at the Equator. Then the train plunges down some 4,000 feet through sugar-cane fields, miles and miles of them. The turns are so sharp that I could see the engine pulling us by poking my head out of the window, for all of the two hours after dawn and until our arrival.

Readers of Elspeth Huxley will know that the pioneers of

Kenya and the British government were considered a little crazy to have started the uneconomic and dangerous scheme to build a railway in the first place. Something like 2,300 men, most of them Indians, were killed in the construction of it, mostly by the Masai, but a few by lions. One railway inspector was dragged out of his carriage by a lion and eaten by the side of the track. That particular carriage now stands in the railway museum at Nairobi. Though the food, dinner and then breakfast, is pretty awful on the train it is a very adventurous journey in its way. It is odd to think that Nairobi was simply a railhead in the middle of a swamp to begin with.

Before I left Nairobi I at last caught up with my hosts. First, the couple who instigated this trip and who offered to lend me their house. They were delightful, and when I said to Mrs Parish you must have been a brave woman to offer a stranger your house, how were you to know I wouldn't burn it down, she simply said, 'I didn't.' My last hosts were present when I stayed with them and they lent me their guest house. It was really wonderful and in the evening they had an open log fire on an open veranda overlooking their garden. Mozart and Beethoven seeped in from the sitting-room, as did the man with the drinks. I met another nice couple in the Muthaiga Club as well this week, called Curtis-Bennet. Mrs Curtis-Bennet offered me a house in the Seychelles. She is the lady who nearly died from swallowing a hornet, and her husband has pancreatitis. Anyway, when she offered me the house, the husband said, 'Over my dead body.' Nevertheless, he bought us all a splendid lunch. And now what with a homeless situation in London and a possible warrant out for my arrest from the Inland Revenue I am thinking quite seriously of living here. Is there life after Kenya?

Ten yards away from me and only a few minutes ago, a large table in this patio bar was surrounded by about ten local girls who were staring and looking at me longingly. No one has done that for 20 years. They stared and they smiled and then they all flaked out and fell asleep. I asked a Kikuyu man sitting next to me for an explanation. He said that they were tired because they had been working all night. Silly me, they were prostitutes. The Kikuyu man, who owns a mere nine acres of maize, three cows, a wife and five children, told me that I could have had my pick for £3.

I have never been much of a coward and although I am apprehensive of AIDS I could never bring myself to make love to a woman who kept a turquoise-blue biro stuck in the bun on the nape of her neck. Sunglasses on top of the head are a bad enough affectation, and the last time I came across that I had to spend the duration reading the Harrods label on the pillow-case.

And now the sun is setting over Lake Victoria and it's orange and above it there are streaks of slate-grey clouds very, very high and not oppressive like English clouds. It gives the impression of this place being vast. It is.

New Haunts

9 January 1988

I am on the move again and I shall very much miss the flat I have been borrowing since last October. Connaught Street behind Marble Arch is a pleasant little village, quiet and still very green at the time I moved in. Summer would be good here with the park being just three minutes' walk away. The pub is quite awful but there is that rarity among shops these days – a fishmonger. Whatever happened to fishmongers? I only know of five in central London. But there is also an old-fashioned butcher's shop, a wine merchant, a dry-cleaner, a supermarket and the best coffee shop – not café – in London. It suffices.

So the next stop is a garret in Covent Garden. I have no objection to attics except for the climbing up to them. My legs said goodbye to me five years ago. I need oxygen to get up to the reading room in the Groucho Club.

But Covent Garden is extremely convenient. It is only a step to the British Museum and the London Library. There are other conveniences too. The ground floor of the house is a betting shop. Next door is a clap hospital. Opposite is a launderette. Fifty yards around the corner is a reasonable pub and near that there is a fish and chip shop. On a clear day you could see the Coach and Horses if it weren't for the houses in the way. No, Covent Garden is all right.

The only thing about it that I can't bear is the new market with its stall-holders who peddle those awful things that come under the heading of 'arts and crafts'. Potters and women with knitted woollen hats who sell nuts make me feel quite ill and I would like to beat them to death with corndollies. Another dreadful thing about them is that they're all so very nice to each other in a rather fey way. I like to see a man come out of his corner when the bell goes. In this weather they keep warm by wrapping copies of the *Guardian* around themselves beneath their coats. They probably keep their babies warm by wrapping them in *New Society*.

It's odd how Covent Garden has become twee. Districts of London have changed in strange ways in recent years. Islington has become self-important, Camden Town intellectual, and the East End has had ideas above its station ever since Richard Wolheim moved there years ago. I think it was he, anyway.

As a schoolboy during the war I lived in Holland Park when I wasn't evacuated to various country places. (Was the Second World War a blessing in disguise for most mothers?) I didn't much like it, but now that it is no longer as huge as it was through a child's eyes I wouldn't mind living there at all. Notting Hill Gate seemed rather seedy then, but that whole area down to Kensington High Street – the most impersonal street in London, possibly? – is now very acceptable.

Holland Park I worked in temporarily as a gardener after I left school and burning autumn leaves was a pleasant way of passing the day but I was scared as a small boy of Holland Walk itself. They said it was haunted by the ghost of a gamekeeper who had been shot there long ago by a poacher. But it is a fact that there was once a racecourse where Ladbroke Gardens now stands. What days they must have been. A day at the races and then a stroll down to Holland House for dinner with the Melbournes, Sheridan and Byron.

The last time I put up in Holland Park was in the Avenue and that was a haunted place as well. Every time I went down to the basement I got as cold as ice at the top of the stairs. I felt someone there. One day the landlady's small son said, 'I saw that man again yesterday.' 'What man?' I asked. 'The man with the tall black hat with a buckle on the front of it.' I suppose he must have been a Regency buck who had had a bad day at Ladbroke Gardens races. It was a Georgian house so it couldn't have been the ghost of a suicidal Puritan. Who else wore buckles on their hats?

And why aren't there any *ordinary* ghosts? I hope that in years to come people will be haunted by ghosts wearing roll-neck sweaters and jeans. Not with their heads under their arms but with rolled-up copies of the *Guardian*. Or the *Sporting Life*.

Clapped Out

23 January 1988

I took my daughter to lunch at the Bombay Brasserie this week and what an excellent place it is. Completely wasted on hordes of sales managers, reps and travellers with shiny trouser bottoms, droopy moustaches, beer guts, a nasty contempt for women, company cars and a fund of bad dirty jokes. There is little more disgusting than a stag gathering. But we had a very good meal in spite of mistakenly picking a dollop of something far too hot from the buffet. There was no cream to go with the fruit salad but I suppose that is something to do with sacred cows.

Over lunch she told me that she wants to emigrate to either America or Australia. I said that I would help her to Australia but not to the States which is far too dangerous for someone too young to be streetwise. Yes, Australia is the place. What the hell is there here and what will be here in ten years' time? Working in Harrods can't be the end of the line. It shouldn't be anyway unless you own it.

But it was a grey, miserable day. We took a taxi up to town where I had to buy some books at Heywood Hill, and what a delight that shop is. Anywhere else would put *Moby Dick* under angling in the sports books shelves. Then we got a taxi to the Groucho Club where we had tea. She regards my excessive use of taxis with some sort of bemused admiration. A treat. In the Groucho she had a slab of white chocolate. She was wearing a black leather jacket and I suppose a motorbike will be the next thing on the shopping list. So I sit here wondering what will become of her and wondering whether I shall ever see her again after I have put her on an aeroplane to Sydney.

In fact I've been awake all night thinking about it, bathed in the light from the wards of the genito-urinary hospital opposite my windows. I have been wondering about the inmates there as well. It strikes some sort of terror in me but it isn't so much the genitals that need love, care and concern as the mind and metaphorical heart. I can see into a ward when their lights are on and I think about them lying there with their bladders up the spout. AIDS, syphilis and heaven knows what else. It is so easy to avoid AIDS. A bottle of vodka a day will do it. A slower train to the same terminus.

After taking Isabel to tea I met an old friend Bill in the pub. We were locked up together in hospital 16 years ago. In those days he drank his way through his furniture, selling everything bar his bed to get the money for a drink. He has been on Perrier for the last three years and I think it is very gutsy of him to come into the pub and buy us a drink without falling off his wagon. He isn't miserable either as are most non-drinking alcoholics. He has had a heart attack since being 'dry' but death can be strangely elusive. Touch wood.

So I sit here in my new home at 4 a.m., thinking about AIDS, Australia, drink and death. I have just drunk six cups of tea and am now switching to a vodka in the hope of getting an hour's sleep. The body clock has gone quite mad. I sleep in the evening and lie awake for most of the night wearing out tapes of Mozart and brooding about all sorts of trivialities.

One of them is whether or not to buy a small microwave oven. Marks and Spencer have started a new line. Red cabbage. Their pre-cooked stuff is so good I am seriously thinking of giving up cooking and living off their food shelves. Perhaps it might make the room stink. I don't know. A Maltese man years ago killed someone in a hamburger joint in Leicester Square by shoving his head in a microwave oven and keeping it there for a minute or two. Another way out, I suppose. And a more harmless Maltese man is coming today to put bookshelves up for me. It is to cost an arm and a leg, timber being the price it is today, but oh, the joy of being reunited with my books. How I have missed them.

And now the clap hospital behind me have just switched on their air-conditioning apparatus and the noise is disconcerting. I drink to their recoveries and wonder do they wonder was it all worth it? Probably. It is extraordinary just what seems to be a good thing at the time. And that has me thinking about racehorses yet again.

Fall Guy

30 January 1988

I had a fall last week that you wouldn't ask a stunt man to perform. I was moving a load of things which was far too heavy for me into my new abode and fell backwards down the steepest staircase I have come across. In fact it is more like a ladder with carpeted rungs. Luckily there was someone in the house who carried me up to my bed. My knee felt as though it had been torn to shreds.

In the morning, repressing screams, I found that I was alone and so had to bump myself down two floors on my bum to phone for help. She arrived with food and drink and a smile of sympathy which also said, 'You can't go on like this.' (Wanna bet?) Then she went off to the Ritz for lunch. I have an electric kettle by the bed and I drank about 15 cups of tea while moaning – I am addicted to the stuff when struck down by whatever – while she ate pheasant overlooking Green Park. Yes, there is justice in the world.

After a while I switched reluctantly, yes, reluctantly, to vodka in the hope it would anaesthetize the leg which was now hurting from hip to toe. It didn't work. I have a high pain threshold but it was sulking. Then a contingent of Samaritans from the Coach and Horses turned up. Bump, bump, bump down three floors to let them in. It is a terrible reflection on one's habits that friends should think you are dead if you fail to appear in the saloon bar for three days.

Anyway, someone phoned Norman to tell him what had happened and apparently he turned round to the pub and screamed, 'He's not dead. He's not dead.' Very embarrassing. Then he turned up swearing about the climb to my garret and bearing various things I can't tell you about for fear of spoiling his reputation for being a shit. He cherishes that. But whenever he thinks the grim reaper is knocking on my door he appears and makes me feel as though I am newly arrived in a manger. If I was in bed with my bride on honeymoon – God forbid – he would interrupt the proceedings by turning up with a bowl of fruit.

But what a mess I am in after four days in bed. The duvet is covered in cake crumbs, tissues, newspapers, an old tea-bag I can't quite reach and the crust of an ex-bacon sandwich. By the side of the bed is a carrier bag into which I have been emptying the ash-tray. It is nearly full. Oddly enough it's rather cosy. It would be a nice wallow but for the pain. And that's receding, although I nearly had a heart attack this morning. What should come through the post from Kenya but a bill from the Muthaiga Country Club. It is for 3,631. I was ice cold for a second. Surely no one could go mad in a club. Of course, it was not pounds but Kenyan shillings. What a nasty turn, though, and it can so often happen to someone with amnesia.

And thereby hangs a tale. The painter Robert McBryde had a grandfather years ago who was boringly and obnoxiously drunk all day and every day. The family got fed up with it and decided on desperate measures. One night, after he had passed out and been put to bed, they pulled back the blankets and poured the entire contents of an Elsan bucket over him, replaced the blankets and left him there. When he came to in the morning they were all standing around his bed shaking their heads sadly and muttering, 'You see, that's what happens to you when you drink.' He never touched another drop and if the story is true, which I doubt, he must have been a very gullible old fool. If I had been in his shoes, perish the thought, I would have gone on drinking and thrown the Elsan away.

Yes, I felt like him for a second or two when the bill from the Muthaiga arrived. They sent the chits I signed as well and 3 and 4 December must have been quite something. I wish I could remember. I also got a chit which says 'Swimming' and I can't swim, but there was a bar by the pool. But how's this chit for laundry: three shirts, five pants, four socks and one pair of jeans for fractionally less than £1. McBryde's grandfather's laundry would have been a little more, probably.

Room at the Top

6 February 1988

I should have known I would end my days in an attic. It has been uphill all the way. Years ago, when I left home, my first bedsitter was in a basement and now by dint of sheer hard work, self-discipline and the limited licensing hours I have raised myself to these lofty heights from where I can gaze into the wards of a genito-urinary hospital.

What is good is that it is wonderfully warm and cosy here. On the one hand I am cut off and on the other I am smack bang in the middle of the West End. There is a very good atmosphere here and there is something vaguely Dickensian about it. For example, it is a suitable room in which to toast muffins. Chatterton wouldn't have been seen dead in it. But, as I sit here chain-drinking cups of tea and eating some chocolate cheesecake Norman gave me, I do wonder how they are going to get the coffin down the stairs. Slide it, probably.

What worries me most, though, is what happens when my friend and landlord's lease runs out. If we all have to leave, that is. Depending on the financial situation the only alternatives I can see are beachcombing in Barbados and taking an overdose of sugar-cane or moving into the Muthaiga Club and becoming the resident bore.

Meanwhile, my Maltese man from the Coach and Horses has done an excellent job putting up bookshelves for me – a simple thing that most people bodge – and tomorrow I shall be reunited with my books, pictures and bed. I expect the bed will look at me reproachfully for having played away matches for a year, unless it too, mercifully, has amnesia. The removal people are to charge me £25 per man per hour. I think that's quite a lot but I wouldn't want to hump anything more than a tea-bag or bottle up here. While they are at it I might get them to tie a rope around the chimney-stack and dangle it to the ground outside my window. If there was a fire downstairs I'd be cooked. And I would prefer to be pickled.

And now my Malteser has just arrived to rewire the place. Monica, the typewriter, will have her very own socket. She didn't like working off car batteries in the park. What I haven't yet told her is that she is going to write a book. How do you break such awful news? She doesn't mind short, sharp bursts but a page a day for nine months isn't a pretty pregnancy. We have been trying for so long to have a baby. If it turns out to be black I shall be rather annoyed.

Be that as it may I have finished the cheesecake, run out of tea-bags and the door bolts are sliding back all over England. Time to go to work. The trouble with this job is that you don't get any holidays. Can you imagine having to talk to Norman's mother about the weather for 365 days a year? People work in coal mines to avoid that. Which reminds me, I got a letter out of the blue the other day from a man I worked with in Handley Deep pit years and years ago. I don't remember him because they all look the same down there but it's nice that people like to keep in touch across the years. If Arthur Scargill catches him reading the *Spectator* while eating his snapping he could be shot-fired. That pit, incidentally, closed now, was 3,000 feet deep, so one has come up in the world: 3,060 feet.

I often wonder what became of the lovable, drunken Poles I lived with in a hostel. They're probably all passed out in the Polish Club in Kensington now if they aren't permanently underground. And whatever became of the big black Jamaican called Winston Churchill who beat me up in the lamp-shed one day?

It is pondering such trivia that drives me down and out of this eyrie for fear of permanently jamming the brain in a time warp. You could end up lying on a bed with a few drinks, reminiscing for the rest of your life, and that is why I shall now go and discuss the seasonal rainfall with Norman's mum. Anything to break this mould of introspection. It is horribly addictive and we are surrounded by things addictive from the very moment we are born. Most of them deadly.

Misspent Time

20 February 1988

This is the sort of thing that comes through the letter-box: 'Dear Sir, I've been reading a few things of yours in *The Spectator*, not a lot but enough to make me wish for meeting you somewhere. That's it, I'm writing you to see (find out?) if you would like to misspend a bit of your time with me. I'm not very interesting, sometimes with a bit of efforts I attain to be, but I have a pair of boots that it can be lace up, up. I'll be looking the post every day since now with my fingers cross and the telephone!! Saluds Muchos, Mari.'

I wrote a similar kind of letter to Veronica Lake when I was 13. But I think Mari probably is interesting although I am not into lace-up boots, blind dates or going all the way over to SE24 for a helping of paella and a flamenco legover. At the bottom of the letter Mari has made a little drawing of a bicycle. I'm not quite sure what that means but whatever it means, I am far too old for that kind of hanky-panky. I need four legs never mind four wheels. Thanks anyway, Mari. It is nice to get a sweet letter.

Some of the letters I get can be quite mad. You would be amazed at the amount of anger a trivial bit of journalism can arouse. Any day now I expect to receive a letter bomb because I smoke. There must be somewhere where people don't give a damn about what you do to yourself. It's probably a toss-up between Lambourn and Bridgetown. And I must go down to Lambourn again in the spring to watch them work the two-year-olds and to see Flo in the Red Lion – England's nicest barmaid. It is an annual treat to see Peter Walwyn's horses on the gallops at the top of the Downs and then to descend to Seven Barrows for breakfast.

The only trouble with Lambourn is that it holds some terrible memories for me and I still have daymares as well as nightmares about some terrible driving incidents ten years ago and the shame of it all is still with me. Never again. At least there are taxis in Newmarket but only one in Lambourn at the last count.

Without a car in Lambourn you could be dead and with one and just the one someone else could be dead.

But I have never taken to Newmarket and I wonder how it became racing's headquarters. I suppose because it is flat and open, but that is why it can be so bloody cold when the wind comes across the Heath from the North Sea. The only things I like about it are the sales – not only fascinating but great social fun – the famous sausages sold in the High Street butchers, Charles St George's princely hospitality, a cocktail with Pauline Lambton and a glass of champagne under trees on the July Course. The last time I was there I went to see Fred Archer's grave in the churchyard. I have two pictures of him on the wall. Such a melancholy-looking man and I don't know quite why but his suicide seems slightly sadder than your run-of-the-mill overdose today.

Opposite that churchyard there is quite a hairy pub. Or at least it was 18 years ago when I was on the *Sporting Life*. Jockeys and stable lads are partial to the occasional punch-up. I have known three who could have taken to the ring instead of the turf. In the old days stable lads boxed to keep fit and the habit has stuck.

I do remember one thing I liked about Newmarket at one time and that was having a drink and passing the time of day with Tommy Weston in the Subscription Rooms. He'd sit there waffling away about the past and I would look at him and think how strange that this little old man rode both Sansovino and Hyperion to win the Derby. He had bundles from Lord Derby in his time, blew it and sadly at the end couldn't go into the Rooms because he was then incontinent.

I once played a game of clock golf there in the garden for £10 a hole with barely a shilling in my pocket and somehow scraped out of that. Hectic days. The editor complained recently about my filing the same column twice from Kenya. On 2,000 Guineas day in 1971 I filed the same column five times to the *Sporting Life* in one afternoon. At the last telephone call the copy-taker said, 'You've been in the Subscription Rooms all morning, haven't you?' Yes indeed.

Places in the Sun *12 March 1988*

Well, I'm off to Thailand today and it will make a change from eating in the Rasa Sayang in Frith Street. I'll be warm tomorrow and I haven't been that since Kenya. The only way I have been able to get any heat through to these old and brittle bones is by soaking in a hot bath for an age, adding hot water every five minutes. I'd live in the bath if I could read in it but the glasses steam up. But it's nice to lie there sipping a contrastingly cold drink and reflecting on past follies.

Why I mention the cold bones is because I am increasingly preoccupied with bad health and the subsequent effect it has on my face. I frighten children in the streets. All of this was rammed home by a BBC camera crew who have been filming me for *Review*. I don't know whether the appearance is more embarrassing or humiliating. Both, I suppose. But at least I no longer have to fight women off, and the only women I speak to now are waitresses and barmaids. But all the time that camera was turning I was thinking about the face and that makes it harder to talk at it off the top of one's head. Excuses, excuses. And what a nice crew they were. The producer is Jake Auerbach, a delightful chap, and his assistant, Rosa, even turned up for the filming we did at Earls Court stadium with a bottle of vodka, a bottle of soda water and a thermos flask full of ice. That is really caring and thoughtful, even if I did give them clues when they filmed me in the eyrie the week before.

Anyway, to get back to the business of Thailand. When I told a man in the pub that I was going there he said, 'Oh, you'll have a marvellous time in Bangkok. They've got some stunning-looking whores there and some wonderful sex shows.' When I told him I wasn't interested he was quite amazed. He said that I must get involved. Why? It's all so boring and we've done all that. He was boring too and he went on and on about it. He obviously thought my attitude was very unmacho. Not one of the boys. You, dear reader, might think it very pompous of me to say so but I think his attitude very childish. I don't have to go half way round the world to get laid and anyway I have a heavy burden of memories to take with me to Bangkok. If I declared them they probably wouldn't let me in. That man probably throws bread rolls at dinner parties and sings rugger songs when he's drunk. Thirty years ago, starting out on the journey to Golders Green, I might have felt differently, but not now that I've hung up my condoms. I am going to Thailand to sit in the sun, nibble at satay, tipple and possibly get shot by bandits. And even if Thailand comes up to my expectations I won't mind coming home.

The Flat starts at Doncaster on 24 March. Soon the questions that have been puzzling racing freaks all winter will be answered. If human beings grew up as quickly as horses it would be very strange to watch them develop almost in front of one's eyes. Speaking of which, my daughter was 18 last week and she too is going to Bangkok on her way to Australia. I sit and think about her and wonder what on earth will become of her and also find it rather strange to think that I may never see her again. Is Australia a land of opportunity? I don't know. This was once and you could have had all the 100–1 you wanted about Psidium before the 1961 Derby. But that's another story. Anyway, I'm not quite sure what opportunity is. If my lot did have it in the 1950s not many of us did a lot with it. Odd to think that a convict ship to Australia was an opportunity of sorts. But I do think it an ill omen that so many Australians flock to a dump like Earls Court. Surely the grass there can't be any greener than theirs. So I shall say goodbye to Isabel very soon, pat her on the head, tell her to take care to herself, not to fall in love with a con man – or any man if she can avoid it – and there you go. It's a funny old life, isn't it? One is always losing something or someone.

Nearly Nirvana

26 March 1988

Bangkok

I think I've cracked it. I may have found the end of the rainbow. It's a village called Bangpar-In on the banks of the river Chaophya 70 kilometres north of Bangkok. In the midst of the usual cluster of riverside houses that look to be floating on water-weeds the boat sets you down at a small jetty and from there it is a step to the one road that the village consists of.

It isn't a lot to look at. The road is very dusty. There are three or four vegetable and fruit stalls, and a few children can hardly be bothered to sell straw hats and postcards to passing tourists in the heat of the afternoon sun. Even the dogs are too exhausted to do anything more than raise an eyebrow at passing strangers. And there it is in the middle of all that, the best bar I have come across in years. I knew at a glance from the outside that it would be. You can sniff out a place like that if you have the nose for it. Mine twitched like a pointer's.

It is a simple oblong room with lazy overhead fans, four large, round teak tables, the circular centres of which revolve to pass the condiments. Each of these tables seats about six people, so it is a case of drinkers and eaters mucking in. There are two big fish tanks. One contains giant prawns and the other very juicy-looking river fish. The door to the kitchen is always open and the smells and the noises of cooking seep into the bar. It smacks of something in an old Hollywood western. It is ageless and yet beneath those old ceiling fans there are two enormous stainless steel refrigerators loaded with all you could want. An old woman wreathed in beatific smiles sits by the door, but her two ravishing daughters do the work. They stretch out like yawning cats when they are not serving and when they are beckoned they slide over the floor to you in their silks, their eyes full of messages.

The tourists went off to see the ruins and I stayed with the coach driver to drink and watch him eat lunch. He had a prawn and vegetable soup, and the lumps of prawn were the size of dumplings. Would you believe 35p? People came and went and one man, having just finished work, sat down with us and drank half a bottle of Thai whisky in ten minutes. A benign fool.

Close to this bar there are a few river houses to rent. There are also regular buses to and from Bangkok. I can see it. Breakfast, a potter about in the garden and tending the indoor plants, a possible paragraph or two and then lunch and dalliance in the bar. My description does not do it justice but never have I come across such ambience. The storks on the river and the birds in the palms scream away and the only other noise is the sizzling of woks and the laughter and, of course, the tinkling of ice in your glass.

Back in Bangkok the next day, I found the other end of the rainbow in a back street off the main business area. Bangkok is blessed with delightful hidden gardens and beautiful houses in the backwaters away from the concrete. I was asked to a lunch party by a Thai interior designer who went to Harrow of all places. We sat in a lovely octagonal open-sided summerhouse by a pond in a lush little garden. Two girls cooked endless bowls of Thai food and Mozart accompanied us (there is an excess of awful pop music here).

The house is a cool, white stone building with teak parquet floors and oddly like one that I know in Elm Park Gardens. The host hardly moves out of it. Fruit and vegetables are delivered every day and with that garden and those cooks there is nothing to go out for. I would like to lie down there and just wait for it.

Cat and Mouse

30 April 1988

The disgusting little cameos of life today that I glimpse with more and more frequency are merging to make a vast and revolting canvas. I have thought a lot about running away recently but even in a jungle or desert I know I would bump into a football supporter, trip over a dustbin liner and hear loud piped music. People stink

Last Sunday in Chapel Street Market I popped into a pub to refuel and had to leave at once. The decibels of the juke-box, the smell of sweat and general filth was too much. Then, outside the pub, half a dozen or so young men wearing Arsenal scarves and sweat-shirts who saw me go into the pub started jeering at me. Their obscene enquiries as to whether the pub wasn't good enough for me and hadn't I got enough money to buy a drink have filled me with gloom ever since. It isn't pleasant to be sneered at and shouted at by yobs. It is irritating when people are stupid but horrific when they are mindless. I don't know what the world is coming to. Well, yes I do, but I wish it would get on with it.

And now the Government and medical profession are urging us to avoid heart attacks if we possibly can. Why? Are we all supposed to be run over by buses or jump off Beachy Head? The yobs I encountered in the market should be encouraged to soak up cholesterol. Their fry-ups and lager should be subsidized. But no. The Government now want to ban death and death is too good for some people. They think that, like smoking, it's bad for you.

But to be fair to this lousy life it has not been quite all gloom. Fair weather and friends alleviate the despondency I feel when I think of the decline and fall of God's empire. Even so there are always minor irritations. Take the service and the bar staff in the Coach and Horses. I have been deer-stalking in Scotland and have walked to within five paces of a gazelle by Lake Victoria but never have I come across so shy a species of animal as the ones Norman employs. When you are in urgent need of a drink they catch your scent and stampede into the kitchen or down to the cellar. They also, like a herd grazing, *all* take their lunch breaks at the *same* time.

The other annoying thing is I have spent all the money I have collected for the Groucho Club Derby Day outing. We might all have to hitch-hike to Pontefract races instead on that day. The Derby coach is now fully subscribed, which means that International Distillers & Vintners Ltd plus a few ethnic restaurants in and around Soho are better off by quite a lot of loot that was supposed to have passed through my hands and not fallen out of them. Yes, the current obsession with ethnic food is something of a mystery to me. Perhaps it started when I was in Thailand. But I think your body tells you what it wants. Thank God I am entirely in accord with mine. It always wants tea and toast as I do at the crack of dawn and then it always gives me an alarm call at 11 a.m. Well, not exactly an alarm call, but certainly a cry for help.

So, what else is new? Not a lot, although She who would once iron 14 shirts at a standing – She has cut it down but has removed the marmalade from my duvet cover – gave me a splendid lunch on Sunday after the scene with the yobs in the market. Steeped in curry, satay and noodles as I have been I had quite forgotten the delight of bread and butter pudding made with cream and then smothered in it. So why can't you get English food in London except in somewhere that's too expensive for daily use, like the Connaught? Food, food. I shovel it in but am nearly down to the bantamweight limit of 8st 6lbs. Norman gave me a piece of cheddar cheese yesterday, presumably in the hope it would sustain me until it was time to write out another cheque, or perhaps he unconsciously considers himself to be cat and me mouse, but you can't live on morsels.

So now I think it is time to take off to the Gay Hussar only pausing on the way at the Coach to pick up the latest writ and frighten the staff. It's awful to have to actually go *hunting* for a drink.

Country Ramble

7 May 1988

I would like to be walking through a wood carpeted with bluebells and listening to a cuckoo at this very moment. As it is I am stuck here in the eyrie and all I can hear is the raucous screech of the seagulls sitting on the roof of the genito-urinary hospital behind me. With the advent of spring and so the window wide open I can even hear the orderlies clearing away the breakfast plates in the men's ward.

But I am not quite sure why I should have woken up missing the country so. The last time I walked through the bluebells, ten years ago, I seem to remember that I was crying. Not surprisingly really, when you consider I was living with someone. So why the sudden nostalgia for the country, I wonder? It may be because of wanting very much to eat and drink alfresco. There have been eight months of restaurants and kitchens and I have felt trapped but for Kenya and Thailand. There is a pub in Berkshire where you can eat on the banks of the river Lambourn and gaze at the water. Rivers and ponds – water in almost any form really – are the perfect accompaniment to daydreaming. So is lying in bed skint for that matter.

The other thing that makes me think of the country is a lovely photograph of two barn owls a reader kindly sent me and which stands on my filthy desk (croissant crumbs, a pint of sour milk and a demand for £3,600). I got to love the barn owl when I lived in Suffolk 20 years ago. There were bluebells there too plus meadows of buttercups by the river, two kingfishers and, it goes without saying, quite a lot of crying as well. I wonder what on earth happened to her? Majorca was the last I heard. But the funny thing is that I have never been really happy in the country for long. What a waste of those cottages. I would dearly like to have one of them back now that I am single and sane. Well, sort of.

I did once have a wife whom I never took to the country and we lasted fairly well until she eventually revealed a certain lack of imagination by going off with my then best friend. Such a boring plot for a story. There was a man in Soho once who had three wives in his time and they all of them in their turn left him for the *same* man. Sinister. Better story though. And speaking of stories this life hasn't got much of a plot any more. Since discovering the bliss of being alone I don't do anything any more. That is to say I do the same damned thing every day and today I feel like swapping the West End for trout streams and daisies in the summer and log fires in the winter. Just a dream. At least I shall see a few blades of grass now that the flat racing season is well under way. But a racecourse littered with torn-up betting tickets and a meal on the pavement outside a Greek restaurant in Charlotte Street isn't quite the same thing as the country, is it?

The nearest thing to it here is a picnic in a boat with my daughter on Regent's Park lake. Sitting there under a weeping willow, dangling a hand in the water, is the nearest I have got to living what I was brought up to think of as being university life. *A Yank at Oxford* made a deep impression on me many years ago. Lots of punting, leather on willow and running up bills at bookshops. I would be grateful if any well-educated reader could tell me whether or not it is like that.

Mind you, a university once came to me. Years ago, I was sitting in the Colony Room club one afternoon when who should walk in but E. M. Forster. I was going through a phase of liking his novels at the time and it was quite a thrill to meet the old man. We then struck up a correspondence. Later the letters he wrote me were stolen by a poet and sold to a bookshop. When I was later told that he had once been seen being dangled out of the window by a man in his King's College rooms I got a real inkling of what I had missed by not going to a university. I wonder if colleagues like Auberon Waugh and Geoffrey Wheatcroft suffered similar indignities.

So, what Oxford and Cambridge never got the cricket pitches and weeping willows of Regent's Park got. That's what I call a bloody bad second. A mood indigo instead of a blue.

Souped Up

28 May 1988

I think I may have to get married again or at the very least employ an au pair girl or a gentleman's gentleman. Being ill in bed without a nurse is hell. Yesterday the effort of getting up to heat up a tin of soup made me nearly faint and I don't exaggerate. The pancreas is an unforgiving bastard. But it has been like going back to childhood. Last night I managed a Marmite sandwich, a banana and a glass of milk and that is precisely what my mother gave me for tea when I was about 12 years old, although bananas were hard to come by then and so it was usually an apple. And I remember jam sandwiches with great affection. Whatever happened to high tea?

It is almost enough to make me feel nostalgic for the Blitz. One was too young to be really frightened and I liked sleeping under the basement staircase, drinking cocoa amid the whistle of bombs and the crack of anti-aircraft guns. When it got really bad my mother took me down to the platforms of Holland Park tube station which reeked of fish and chips and vinegar. My mother also used to make very good Spanish omelettes with dried egg powder. The other standby, coupons permitting, was pilchard pie which I wouldn't give any thanks for today. But they were happy days in a way. There was no need for money, no knowledge of sex and no urgency for a drink. You see what happens when you start to grow up and the Germans surrender. You start going mad.

But the last few days have been exhausting. Why it should be so tiring just lying in bed sipping tea or soda water and smoking cigarettes is a mystery to me. It took me half an hour to dress this morning and crawl to the desk. Still it's better than being in hospital, not that you can get into one any more thanks to the collapse of the Health Service. I need to go back to the

Middlesex to get restabilized but it's like trying to get into Eton. I should have put my daughter down for it ten years or so ago.

And talking of hospital I am worried about the one behind me. It has an enormous air conditioner outside it and I have had to close the bedroom window for fear of Legionnaires' disease. I have become a little preoccupied with that since the outbreak at and via the BBC. You can hardly move these days without catching something and it is essential that I must be well for my wretched birthday this Friday and for next Wednesday, much more important, Derby Day.

I dread still being stuck here in bed on the great day itself sipping tomato soup between moaning. Our party is having poached salmon and salad followed by strawberries and cream plus afternoon tea after and I'm sure there will be some interesting rows as the champagne takes effect. What I do think is a little sad is that the great man won't be there. No doubt the warders will allow him to watch the race on the television screen but dear oh dear how the mighty have fallen. He is smiling at me now from the wall above the desk and I find it depressing. Such jolly days on the crest of endless waves.

Meanwhile I shall have to go back to bed with a raspberry sandwich and a pot of tea and take a Valium. Dreadful things. I still have a hangover from the one I took 15 hours ago. Next week I hope to be more *compos mentis* when I address you.

With One Eye Open *11 June 1988*

The combined Groucho Club and Coach and Horses Derby Day outing went very well considering the crew and the fact that the first champagne cork popped at 7 a.m. The Groucho laid on a very good breakfast which was eaten in a strange hush. Everyone seemed to be out of context at that time of day, caught, as it were, with their guards down. It even took a couple of hours for Norman to move from depression to mania.

When we did finally get to the course he – who doesn't know the difference between 6–4 and Marble Arch – had a silly argument with a bookmaker. I crept off for a few minutes with She who would once iron 14 shirts at a standing – She can hardly bring herself to massage my back any more – to have a drink with Robert Sangster. As befits a man with a few shillings in his current account he exuded a calm confidence. He is not the sort of man who would jump out of his skin if he heard a knock on his door. Anyway, his confidence or whatever was a little infectious so I plunged rather too heavily on his Glacial Storm just as they were being loaded into the stalls. Here endeth the umpteenth lesson. I didn't before realize that the West Indies or Bangkok were only one and a half lengths away. Oh well.

After an excellent Groucho lunch of salmon and strawberries the resident Coach and Horses eccentric, the Red Baron, passed out on the grass. A patrolling posse of policemen examined him quite closely to make sure he wasn't dead. He wasn't and lived to eat yet another lunch. What I thought was a little odd was the fact that the eye over which he wears his monocle was wide open. I have seen a man asleep standing up in the Colony Room Club but never a man unconscious with an eye open.

But the day's punting revealed two people to be very crafty gamblers: *The Spectator*'s Christopher Howse and Quartet Books' Stephen Pickles. My brother Bruce backed the winner and he still hasn't bought me a drink. My brother Oliver lost and I have just sent my bookmaker, Victor Chandler, a cheque which I hope he takes like a man. It took one to write it out. But still, when I won £800 on Grand National day his cheque to me came winging its way through the post at the speed of light. British Post Office light. We must be all square come the day of the King George VI and Queen Elizabeth Diamond Stakes when hopefully Glacial Storm and Kahyasi might renew their rivalry.

It must be said, by the way, that the two young men and two young women from the Groucho who served the drinks and the food were bloody marvellous and nowadays nobody wants to serve anybody. But there was a strange end to a jolly but expensive day. She who would once iron went home and who should walk into the pub but that heroine of yesteryear whom I haven't seen in ages – She who would once drown in my eyes. As it happens she is now trying to drown herself in the eyes of a publican I have known for years. Better a publican's eyes than a hack's. She is still a mess, sadly, and she was wearing the dress I think I once cleaned my shoes with in 1983.

A pity really because I thought she would change and settle down, as my number four used to say.

So, another Derby has passed and very soon we shall be working on the puzzle of the 1989 Derby winner. We haven't seen him out in public yet, I'm sure of that. So where is he lurking? I would love it to be in Peter Walwyn's yard. Oh for the days of 1975 and Grundy and the sun over the yard-arm of the Seven Barrows yard. An adjustable yard-arm. Peter recently had an arm smashed by a horse, the good Major Dick is in a wheelchair and the hero Fred Winter isn't as well as he deserves to be. Why don't these things happen to the shits? The Ayatollah Khomeini still lives.

And another thing that depresses me is Lester having his OBE stripped. I find that the entire business of that man's life being screwed up by his silly greed terribly sad. It is almost as though Nelson struck his colours. Meanwhile, keep an eye on those two-year-olds. Next year we must win, keep the Red Baron awake and gag Norman after 10 a.m. And now to hospital to be restabilized. I shall study form for a week.

The Joy of Nursing *18 June 1988*

The hospital I am in is unique. In the middle of the sticks and in the Avon area, it was originally built as an American army/air force base. The 30 wards and other buildings were barrack rooms and so Ward 17 is like an elongated bungalow. I am lucky enough to have a room of my own, a side ward, and there is a patio out at the back, flowers and a sprinkling of garden furniture under a small unidentified tree. Yesterday I was sitting there in the sun nursing a drink and for a moment I could have been on holiday until a nurse approached with a syringe asking for blood. I still felt as though I was on holiday. It was really no worse than a French waiter approaching with the bill.

I thought you might be surprised at the fact that I was nursing a drink on hospital territory, but the business of having the diabetes restabilized here is like nothing I have known in the big city hospitals. I suggested that it was ridiculous to take a man out of his environment, change his way of life and metabolism and get the balance of insulin still correct after being discharged and disgorged into Soho again. That is like twisting a graph. The good boss here agreed with me and that is why I am sipping a vodka on the patio.

The nursing staff are very caring. Yesterday evening the ward sister glanced at the bottle on the top of my bedside locker and, looking most concerned, asked me, 'Mr Bernard, are you *sure* you're drinking enough?' You could marry a woman who talks like that.

The other reason for being here, other than being restabilized, is to gain some weight and strength. Ten days ago in London I had to ask a man to help me across Shaftesbury Avenue. I felt so weak and feeble I thought that if I fell down in the road I would drown in the traffic. So they are stuffing me like a Strasbourg goose here. At lunch yesterday a nurse ticked me off for not eating more ice-cream with the strawberries a visitor brought me. The improvement has been remarkable and rapid. The belt has had to be loosened a notch. I am not yet doing cartwheels or handsprings on my way to the patio but at least I don't have to hang on to the walls for support as I walk.

There is a rather odd night sister of Sicilian extraction on Ward 17. She rebuked the sweet thing who looks after me during the hours of darkness yesterday. Apparently she told the Sweet Thing, 'Don't come on duty wearing that perfume again. You'll excite him.' Could perfume be a medical breakthrough. I wonder? Brought back to life by Chanel or Joy?

Apart from my own boring case there is the usual collection of oddballs that is always to be found in a hospital ward. The ones I go to anyway. There is a 19-year-old boy who was stabbed in a fight in Bristol. It seems to have affected his mind as much as his guts, but he was obviously in some sort of trauma before that. Now he is nearly gaga and it's very sad to see. Colin has a frightening hole in his head where he was operated on because of a tumour. He seems quite OK but come the evening he is lost in every sense of the word. I watched the first day of Royal Ascot with the 'Colonel'. He, poor chap, is a total physical mess. He groans terribly and a lot of his groans coincided with the finishes of races and you might have thought that he was losing fortunes.

But I had to bite my tongue right off yesterday to stop myself from laughing and thereby being accused of being a racist. A giant of a black man, built on the lines of a Joe Frazier or Mike Tyson, was admitted wearing an oxygen mask. He looked to be spark out. Just as I was about to hold his hand and offer him words of good cheer and comfort he suddenly whipped off the mask, leant over to his locker, grabbed a banana and ate it in two gigantic bites. We are now sharing my oranges but not my vodka.

It's a funny thing this business of being allowed to drink in hospital. It seems to mystify the nurses. They aren't exactly whispering in corners about it, but they are certainly puzzled. Could that be why they are treating me so well? One of them has seen me on television so I get a little VIP treatment for that as well. They are all lovely, the one exception being the solitary male nurse on the ward. I don't like male nurses. They are like ducks out of water and not nearly as funny. This chap is a parsimonious, judgmental prig. I asked him to bring me in some cigarettes on his next shift and he screamed like a poof who has suddenly and unexpectedly been groped. He said, 'I couldn't possibly. I deeply disapprove of smoking. You've asked quite the wrong person,' and off he swept. Why does the medical profession attract so many judgmental people? The good doctor here doesn't keep telling me what's good for me, but then he is a *Spectator* reader.

Right-hand Man

25 June 1988

Last Saturday afternoon I went with a friend into the Mecca betting shop in Greek Street to listen to a race commentary. I had a financial interest in the event and was anxious to hear how my money would run. I heard very little of the race thanks to a man who was making a lot of noise watching a football match from Germany on television. I remonstrated with him, pointing out to him that a betting shop was primarily a place for horse and greyhound racing punters and not one for football freaks and yobs. At that he asked me to step outside and I did.

That was my first mistake. You should never accept such an invitation or make it. Either you walk away from the situation or you hit your man immediately and as hard as you can. It would be understating the case to say that I am a trifle ring-rusty. I am on the scrap-heap. But I went outside on to the pavement with him noting that he was probably 2 lb lighter than a cart-horse. The second mistake was to think. It is amazing how many things you can think of in a split second and in a split second I was mulling over matters concerning street fights. It occurred to me that if I began by jabbing a left on to his nose it might disconcert him somewhat and bring tears to his eyes, putting me into soft focus. It was during these considerations that he caught me flush on the chin with a right-hander. I have been hit harder. The punch didn't matter. What did was my head hitting the pavement. It made a sickening noise like two coconuts being banged together and the pain nearly made me vomit. I thought I might lie there for three weeks.

Now I have seen a lot of the police in my time, usually an unwelcome sight, but on this occasion they appeared quite miraculously out of their blue. Shades of the US Cavalry in the last reel. There was a uniformed policeman and an unmarked squad car which must have been cruising Soho on the look-out for drug dealers. My opponent was bundled into the car and was nicked. My head hurt so much I thought of taking it to hospital for an X-ray but it recovered slowly over a couple of drinks in the Ming Chinese restaurant. All that hurts now after four days is a pelvic bone, seeing as how my flesh now no longer acts as a cushion. My friend went off to Vine Street police station to make a statement and I kept hearing echoes of the skull hitting the pavement. The manager of the betting shop, I heard later, had telephoned for the police at the 'off' and so thanks to him. I would not fancy his job. There are some dodgy customers in that shop but he can't help that. But the man who put me on the pavement was, I am pretty sure, a stranger on the manor. He looked like one of those people who can start a fight in an empty room and I wonder what he got when he came up to face the beak on Monday.

I had resolved shortly after being lifted to my feet to fight only women and children from now on, but something much more frightening than the man with the right hand marched into the Coach and Horses the following day. A gang – that is the only word – a gang of 12 lesbians walked in throwing out challenging glances at us poor men nursing fractured skulls or hangovers. I find lesbians really rather frightening. They do actually *hate* you whereas men like the right hand merely want to duff you up. That is pretty mindless of them but it is not as awesome as hate. Not much is.

In a strange way I would quite like a return with the right hand if I was equipped with a large spanner or a car starting handle which was a favourite weapon in the 1950s. No, I wouldn't. He might just possibly be okay and I know how nasty I can be in circumstances which involve something as trivial but irritating as asking someone to switch off the television or turn it down. I could have hit the Colonel over the head with the television set in the day room of the hospital last week if he had looked as though he would live to see the *News at Ten*.

Well, to be a mite realistic I don't think that Saturday was the last occasion on which I shall be whacked but at least I shall bob and weave a bit the next time I come out of this unlucky corner. And to think that 30 years ago I liked to hear the call 'seconds out' followed by the bell. Both the bell and the bell for last orders are to be dreaded now.

Night Thoughts

2 July 1988

As I write to you it is five hours, 12 cups of tea and 20 cigarettes since Mike Tyson took just 91 seconds to knock out Michael Spinks and I feel whacked too. The only sleep I seem to get nowadays is the five minutes in a restaurant snatched between the pudding and the bill. Anyway, even if I were not an insomniac the noise of the air extractor and that of the staff dropping test tubes and phials containing what can only be nitroglycerine which emanates from the genito-urinary hospital beyond the window would prevent any rest. What's more I've got two people coming for supper tonight and I shall be in no condition to make toast by then, never mind create what the Notting Hill Gate branch of Lyons way back in 1949 rather strangely had on their menu billed as Chicken *à la Poulet*. (They also had Mushrooms *sur* Toast.)

But what about Mike Tyson's neck? Nineteen and three-quarter inches! I don't trust people who use exclamation marks but that man has to have them. He is a very workmanlike fighter, don't you think? Thank God he wasn't in the Greek Street betting shop last Saturday week. My head has healed from that one-punch fracas but the crack the pavement gave it seems to have exacerbated the two cysts, one behind each ear, that I have had for a while. They are now the size of plums. They embarrass me, make me feel self-conscious and to some extent they alarm me. Either they are there because the wretched pancreas can't break down fat any more or Norman is poisoning me.

By the way, he took his virago to see *Aida* and when I asked him what he thought of it he simply said, 'I couldn't understand a f———ing word of it,' and returned his attention to the till. The Eton boating song he can grasp. The virago herself, being Italian, explained it to him though and told him that it wasn't being sung in Egyptian.

Anyway, yesterday in the Coach and Horses I was sipping a drink and thinking with an affection that has strangely increased over the years of Mrs Bernard III when I was tapped on a cyst and turned round and who should it be but she, who had blown in from Spain. Shortly after that our daughter blew in. It was all – how shall I put it – very *nice*? But then, shortly before Mike Tyson put that neck of his through the ropes in Atlantic City, I wondered if cysts, wasting, diabetes and all the other awful indications of decay might not be the rottenness of 20 years ago coming out like pus from a lanced boil. I can't help pondering such things at 2.30 a.m. I should have been better to them and Michael Spinks should have distanced himself from Tyson with a bit of use of the left jab. What should have been is a heavy load and a nuisance thing to think about.

Oh well, today is going to be splendid. I shall go out soon, have a cocktail and listen to some really ridiculous remarks about the big fight from people who have absolutely no idea or conception of what it is like to be in a boxing ring with someone who is being paid to hurt you, and then go and have a nap in the blueberry pie in the Groucho Club before getting what may be the last supper together. That may not sound a lot of fun to you and you're right. It isn't to me either. I had intended to get out of this dreadful part the agent in the sky got me and go to Spain for a few days to drown in the sun, but trouble with air traffic controllers put paid to that one.

News of all that I heard on LBC Radio and why, I would like to know, do nearly all the women who read and announce news on the radio speak with what must be called Tesco accents? Only the stunning Jill Pyrer can speak as though she is not at the end of a queue. It could be that Tesco talk is the result of the heady climb from suburbia to media. To desert the telephone for the microphone is a giant step in any woman's life. Years ago, Margaret Thatcher probably had quite a nice voice.

And now it is six hours since the big fight and my daymares in the night and I have suddenly got a pain in the region of my spleen. Poor Michael Spinks must have a pain in the head and please don't tell me that there is always someone worse off than yourself.

Best of Three

9 July 1988

I received a letter last week containing a first-class return ticket to Birmingham and a scribbled note of instructions. I was to get the 19.10 from Euston and have dinner on the train and on arrival get a taxi to the Central Television studios. A room had been booked for me at the Holiday Inn and the following morning a car would take me to Henley-in-Arden. Well, I thought, how jolly good of my friend Michael Elphick to fix up for me to spend the weekend at the hotel he has a share in at Henley-in-Arden, which is where he hangs out when he is not filming episodes of *Boon*.

So I got to the studios and was taken into a room full of people drinking. I thought it must be the *Boon* production office throwing a party for Michael but I couldn't see him. After a few drinks – and I had already had a few on the train – a woman came up to me and told me it was time to start. Start what? The show. It dawned on me, the penny dropped rather heavily, that I was in a chat show starring George Best. The subject of the chat was alcoholism. Why had they sorted me out? Appropriately I could see three George Bests. He, poor chap, said he hadn't had a drink now for two months. I hadn't had one for five minutes. So endeth the first night in Birmingham in the middle of which I was very sick indeed. Avoid hospitality plonk.

In the morning I tried to get stuck into an enormous breakfast but it was a fry-up. Ugh. Then I was driven to the White Swan in Henley-in-Arden. No Elphick. I sat at the bar with *The Times* picking losers and took refreshment. It was beginning to be an odd weekend. Then Michael appeared looking surprised to see me. I asked him, 'You were expecting me, weren't you?' No. Another penny dropped rather slowly. Michael has often asked me to the White Swan but he hadn't on this occasion. Obviously Central Television had telephoned me at the wrong end of my working day, probably at the Coach and Horses, and I must have said that I would go on the chat show if they would ferry me over to Henley-in-Arden.

Anyway, Michael had to open two garden fêtes that afternoon and then whizz off to Chichester to see his mum. I came back to London later reflecting that it was a long way to have been to have had a jar with Boon. Oh well. A strange mix-up. Quite obviously the demon has burned up all my memory cells. I am now wondering if I have ever been on television without knowing it. But I hope the children in Birmingham stayed up to watch the show. It must have warned them. I mean you wouldn't look forward to having a face like this.

But of the three George Bests I saw I like the first one best. The one in the hospitality room. A nice chap. I did actually interview him at the height of his fame ages ago. He turned up in the Trattoria Terrazza with three girls which I thought was showing off a little. But now I am having second thoughts about it. Perhaps there was only one girl and perhaps I had had some hospitality of sorts before our meeting. If ever another invitation comes my way to appear on television I shall turn up wearing an eyepatch. Can you imagine seeing three of a man like Terry Wogan?

So back in London today I have just got a letter with another invitation. This one is from the officers' mess of the 1st Battalion Welsh Guards asking me if I would like to have dinner with them and then speak to them. They must be bonkers. After-dinner speech-making is not my forte but yes, Marcus Scriven – rank and number please – I should be delighted. The last time

I was in an officers' mess, 14/20 Kings Hussars, I was scrubbing the floor. The news that your commanding officer was educated (?) at Pangbourne is rather alarming. Does he cane you for talking after lights out? You say the CO expects me to stimulate and entertain him with my eloquence. Well, I would have a shot at it at breakfast time, but after dinner I am about as eloquent as a pudding. You have been warned.

Summary Discharge *16 July 1988*

At last. This coming Tuesday I have an appointment with a surgeon who hopefully will cut out the cysts on the back of my head and neck. They are beginning to hurt like hell and I never thought the time would come when I would actually look forward to an operation. The other thing at the back of my head apart from bilateral lipomata is the thought that they may find something worse in there. Could it be a book? Possibly. I feel like an old dust-jacket.

Anyway, the good doctor who looked after me in Bristol has had the courtesy to send me a discharge summary. I liked that. Usually doctors want to keep your body a secret from you. It makes them feel more powerful that way. The summary says, 'History: this 56-year-old man was admitted for stabilization of his diabetes. He had been insulin dependent for 12 years but had recently been neglecting himself. He has chronic pancreatitis and had had severe diarrhoea with weight loss and muscle wasting recently. He also has a high alcohol intake.' On examination, 'He had a fine tremor at rest, obvious muscle wasting palmar erythema and spider naevi. His pulse was 70/regular. BP, 140/90. Heart sounds normal and minimal peripheral oedema. His chest was clear and he had a smooth liver edge palpable to two cms.' Nobody could ask for a better epitaph than 'He had a smooth liver edge palpable to two cms.' I am also rather pleased with having a *fine* tremor as opposed to one of the awful ones with which you can not have a saucer with your cup of tea for fear of the noise. But even with the cysts and dead pancreas I have to think that I am living in a miracle of physical engineering.

But anyway doctor, I am taking the capsules and eating three times a day. Book matches are remarkably useful as they tell me where I had dinner. This morning for breakfast I had two Marks & Sparks salmon fish cakes followed by some raspberries and cream washed down by a pint of milk, later to be chased by a vodka and orange juice which is as good a way of taking vitamin C as I know. I have also stopped smoking when I am unable to see across the room. And talk about seeing, I got a hell of a fright yesterday when I woke up in the Groucho Club. I thought I was going blind but it turned out to be salad dressing on my reading glasses which I use for eating too as I don't like food to be out of focus. Mind you, pasta and chop-suey are always out of focus whatever you are wearing. I wonder if the Red Baron who comes into the Coach and Horses wears his monocle when he is eating. If he doesn't, then one end of a sausage, say, would be out of focus. A passing thought, but such things worry me in the middle of the night.

And talking of the middle of the night, my landlady has just told me that my room, the eyrie, is haunted. She has heard a typewriter when there is no one there. A writer once did live in it, I know, but could it be that my Monica electric de Luxe has learned to turn herself on? I wish she would stuff some paper in herself when I am not there and get on with it. But I never thought I would end up living with a ghostwriter. On the other hand why not? I have lived with everything else apart from a Booker Prize winning Eskimo, lesbian feminist. Still, with the skill of my doctors even that could come to pass.

And now I must try and get served. It gets harder and harder every day. Norman has always made a point of employing goons in limbo but he played his ace this week. The new barman is a boy who has never before served a drink and who cannot speak a single bloody word of English. Mind you, all of that applies to Norman himself but you'd think he'd get somebody aware of the urgency or emergency. The service is now so slow that the only people you ever see drunk in the Coach are people who have had a skinful at home before they venture forth. As a matter of fact it is just that that has revealed many people to be secret drinkers. I find it rather embarrassing. Particularly when it is a woman. They're so vulnerable aren't they, bless them. All that running eye make-up.

Nicked Again

23 July 1988

One day last week I thought my luck had changed. I was sitting alone at the bar stroking a drink with a swizzle-stick when an extremely attractive young black woman walked in from the Greek Street end of the pub. I didn't stare but I took note. After a couple of minutes, Michael the barman came over to whisper in my ear that she wanted to see me. I cleared my throat, smoothed my hair, walked over to her and said hallo. She asked me was I Jeffrey Bernard, and, reaching for my autograph signing pen and contorting my mouth into a sickly smile, I told her that indeed I was. At that she said, 'I'm from the Inland Revenue,' and she thrust a piece of paper into my hand demanding £3,668.22 within seven days.

You know it's an odd thing, years ago, not that long ago actually, that would have been like a punch to the solar plexus. Nowadays such things simply make me feel slightly numb. Even the smile froze on my face and I was still smiling when Norman came back from Marks & Sparks with the cottage pie. Yes, she was a very nice looking lady indeed. I had another drink of course and pondered the 22p.

Where do they get these strange figures from? More to the point, how on earth did the messenger of ruin know I would be in the Coach and Horses? Either the Collector of Taxes reads the *Spectator*, probably posing as a student in order to get a cheaper subscription rate, or I was grassed, and if I was I know by who. Never mind. We must all pay our taxes. So the seven days is nearly up and I must go and see them tomorrow.

Anyway, I just thought you might like to know that this is the third time I have been nicked in the Coach. The first time was for criminal damage – kicking a car that someone aimed at me – and the last time was for the illegal betting nonsense. What will it be next as a magistrate once dreamily inquired of me? I do think though that fines should be tax-deductible although I must admit that the unprovoked attack on the rubber plant in the Taj Mahal restaurant deserved punishment.

Which reminds me. I heard from the police that the man who

flattened me outside the betting shop was fined £100 and I am sure you think it was worth it. Norman probably paid it for him.

No, that's not fair. He's very good to me and his concern about my muscle-wasting has got him forcing cottage pies and fish cakes down me every day, and speaking of health I went to see a surgeon yesterday about the cysts at the back of my head. He said that to remove them would require major surgery and that it would be a very difficult operation anyway and one that could lead to future complications as well. So I'm lumbered with a couple of bumps which, please God, don't get any bigger. On the credit side they will probably act as cushions in further demolishings outside betting shops. If only they were on my arse I'd be able to sit down.

Well, after the surgeon had washed his hands of me I strolled down to the pub and found two birthday boys there. It was very jolly. Norman ran out to the pâtisserie and bought two incredible birthday cakes and we all had sticky fingers. By the way, the till broke down on Monday (overheating?) and had to be taken away for repairs. Have you ever seen a racemare when her foal is taken from her? It is horribly sad. The staff had to jot down the takings on a scrap of paper which was almost beyond most of them, and it had Norman pacing up and down behind the counter like Wackford Squeers.

Anyway, I've had enough of doctors, pubs, surgeons and Soho for a while and I am going off for a week if the Inland Revenue don't confiscate my passport tomorrow. She who would once iron 14 shirts at a standing has driven down to the South of France and I shall go and see her. I shall go by train since every other way of travel seems to be disaster prone. In a way I am rather surprised that I have never been involved in a disaster although I found the soda water to be flat a moment ago. I do love trains but I don't have happy memories of French railways. I once took a train from Paris to Barcelona and had to stand all the way because three French yobs told me what I could do with my reservation. Yes, the French have them too. So I shall have one for the road and bid a fond farewell to £3,668.22. Especially the 22p.

Lunching with Greene

6 August 1988

Antibes

One of the fringe benefits of dying is that the journey to heaven is not via Heathrow. A harrowing place. It is very crowded here too. It was a mad time of year to come here but to have spent as much time as I have with Graham Greene has not only been a privilege but a delight. But first I went to see She, *sans* ironing board, in Haut de Cagnes. I was trapped there for three days in the square at the top of that small mountain town since my legs could not cope with the amazing steepness of the streets. An attractive prison though, and She cooked some good omelettes with salads which we ate on a balcony with a splendid view to the sea also appreciated by swifts and house-martins, bats homing in at dusk. The cloud with that silver lining was the heat of the nights. I was stuck to the sheets and no shower but just a wash basin. Then She drove me to Antibes before driving herself home.

I do not quite know what to make of this place, the ice-cream capital of the world. The Vieille Ville has charm and a food market that made me long for it to be possible to cook in a hotel room. But is it a posh Blackpool? The boats in the Port Vauban, sleek layabouts, certainly were not earning their keep. I like a scruffy, working fishing boat or two. And what a gritty lot the French here are although they show great compassion for their wretched dogs.

Then I met Mr Greene for a drink at the appointed bar, Félix au Port. I was apprehensive. People who excel in their craft – especially to the extent that he does – tend to make me feel slightly ridiculous. Thank God, however, the Grand Old Man is not in the slightest bit grand. The drink turned out to be an excellent and friendly lunch. Incidentally, I noticed that he sat with his back to the view which he says enhances the restaurant. We lingered over 'the one' for two hours and then he was kind enough to help me find a hotel. We said goodbye and that, I thought, was that.

The next day, he rang me to invite me to his flat for a drink. That surprised me. On arrival he presented me with his new book and a tube of vitamin tablets which he said with sad but twinkling eyes would give me 'the courage to go on'. Yes, he is funny too. After some excellent vodka – it seems that we are both moderately addicted to the stuff – he took me to lunch in a piss-elegant restaurant. He said he had been too lazy to go out to buy some smoked salmon. He said he did not like the restaurant much, it being 'no good for short stories'. I saw his point but it was a very good meal if not simplistic. But he said he did know several good 'short story' restaurants. Furthermore, he suggested I attempt the short story. It was tremendously gratifying that he should have taken the slightest notice of a single word in this column. Yesterday we had lunch again, this time in a 'short story' restaurant. I would very much like to see what his *novel* restaurants in Cuba and Indonesia must have been like in times gone by.

Now, sitting here waiting for the clock to tick to another lunch with him the noise of the traffic is horrendous. The waiter is aggressive and the ice melts at an almost visible speed. But the sun, like sleep when you can get it, is a great healer. Yesterday I lay in it for a few hours. I went up to Roquefort Les Pins to a lovely spot of a hotel to have lunch and play *boules* with two old friends from the Lambourn valley. I could get hooked on *boules*. Some already are. I was told by one of my friends that he was watching Yves Montand playing that game. When he spoke he was asked to be very quiet. 'They are playing for 40,000 francs,' he was told. It would be good were it easier to get a game of *boules* in England. I have only seen it played there once and that was in the back yard of a restaurant in Wimbledon. Who knows, perhaps there are *boules* hooligans here.

Anyway it has certainly been Graham Greene week. Very memorable, even for an amnesiac. Another lunch with him today and then farewell cocktails this evening. At 83, Graham Greene, 27 years my senior, makes me feel like a burnt-out case. I shall miss him.

Parting Shots

20 August 1988

Another good man has died. Jimmy Collier owned probably the best hotel in England, the Bibury Court Hotel, a beautiful place and he gathered a very rich mix of people to it. During the week of the Cheltenham National Hunt Festival the roof would come off. He was a very good cook too and I shall miss him for much more than the fact that he used to let me stay there for nothing. He made life fun. A bit of a lark. It was very good to sit beside the trout stream that runs through the garden and contemplate between the rounds.

And now I contemplate the friends who have died over the past ten or 15 years. Who on earth is going to replace them? I really cannot see any *young* people about to fill the shoes of lost friends and I find that depressing. True there is a metaphorical queue lining up to become a 'Soho character' and another to become 'Jack the Lad' but they don't have a lot of style about them in my eyes. Sitting here at my table I am beginning to feel like General Custer and there isn't an Indian in sight. Everybody over the age of 50 is a Custer. Nearly a third of the people in the framed photographs on the walls of this room are dead. And now I've run out of Perrier water. It is all one hell of a struggle. But enough of that. What have we today?

Well, there is lunch with a lady and then an extremely promising horse runs at York this afternoon. I can hardly be bothered to get up and dress for them. The carrots God dangles for this ass don't get any bigger. The weather forecast is good though so I shall go out and get 500 yards of it. But have the grouse been flown down yet to more humble establishments than the Savoy? I like a grouse as you know but I can't stand game potatoes which make me think of posh chips.

Humble pie is another nasty dish but they should put it on the menu in the Groucho Club for the media people. I have watched and heard a lot of that mob being interviewed recently and it is not a pretty sight or sound. The interview, like going to the lavatory or reading poetry, should be as private as possible. All the journalists who conduct these interviews are young women from women's magazines and media journals who sit on the edge of their chairs, pencil poised above a writing pad on their knees, looking horribly eager and sickeningly sincere. That is their picture of journalism. The career women being interviewed don't half raise their voices when they come out with phrases like, 'We're going into production next week,' or, 'My New York publisher has told me go for it.'

I watched an interview last week that lasted *all* afternoon. I know it can be quite attractive to talk about oneself – it does not require any thinking – but an entire afternoon is a bit much. It is even more annoying that I have nothing better to do than eavesdrop an interview for three hours. What I do like to eavesdrop is a series of recriminations between a couple having a tiff. I like the vibrant hiss through clenched teeth which can sometimes sound like a weird oriental musical instrument being plucked. The word, sick, in the well-known phrase and saying, 'You make me *sick*', is a frightening sound taught, I suspect, in most girls' schools.

Yes, I am sure they have talking classes as well as singing classes in girls' schools. For example it is essential to be able to get the right modulation, intonation and implication into the query. 'And where do you think you're going?' And a bit of jollity in a parting shot is essential as when a wife going off to work one morning put her head round the bedroom door and said to me, 'Don't forget to get drunk today, will you?' The worldweariness in someone else's voice who once said, 'You've snapped at me for the last time,' put me in mind of the last groan of an enormous animal dying.

As for 'You've been drinking,' that can be made into a statement, an educated guess or an enquiry by slight and subtle shiftings of the vocal chords. Women can also get a tremendous amount of mileage and meaning out of, 'Can we go home now please?' It is wonderful to be no longer a sounding board for this stuff. All I get now from She is a businesslike, 'Have you remembered to take your insulin?' How I long to make somebody *sick* again.

Ice Cold in Lambourn

27 August 1988

I returned to Lambourn valley last weekend with some trepidation. The place holds some bad memories for me. Four car crashes and one wife crash. As it turned out it was a delightful weekend and half of it was strangely triggered off by a tragedy. On Monday there was a memorial service for the jockey Paul Coucher who was killed in a car crarsh. It meant that everybody turned out for that and so there was one hell of a thrash in the Swan and the Ibex. All the old faces, some of them with a few more broken veins, but all very jolly.

But the goings-on in Lambourn haven't changed much since I lived there as far as I could see. I had missed a spectacle by a few days. An old friend had, I was told, been given a tremendous whack by someone he had been rude to and was sent flying across a table and some chairs. He lay on the floor with blood pouring from his nose and Wally Swinburn – Shergar's ex-jockey – who doesn't like the sight of blood ministered to him by trying to push ice cubes up his nostrils to stem the flow. I suppose you could put an ice cube up a cow's or horse's nostril if you felt so inclined but up a man's nostril is stretching things a little. I also met a young racing blade who I was told has just asked one of the local bank managers for a loan of £6,000 on top of his outstanding overdraft. The manager said, 'Six thousand! But your overdraft is already more than my annual income.' The man said, 'Well, why don't you get another job?' He got his £6,000.

On Monday afternoon six of us played *boules* in the sunshine and drinks were served. Everything in the valley has got better. Dear old Flo who used to work in the Red Lion has just had an operation to remove a cataract and her heart stopped in the middle of the business. Like everyone else who has died for a short while she said she saw a tunnel and there was a man at the end of it. I asked her hopefully, 'Did he have a drink in his hand?' She said that she hadn't noticed so it is still all a mystery.

The guvnor of the George died quite recently and his wife

has taken up ballroom dancing, her hair quite 'gold with grief'. The Ibex has improved too since Colin Browne has taken over. He used to ride the great Desert Orchid. And now that Noel Bennet has got the Swan it is probably the best country pub I can think of. Fresh turbot on a Sunday and you can actually get served which is proving to be damn nigh impossible here in Soho. Yes, being in Lambourn I missed the celebrations Monday when the new drinking law came into being. I'm told they let off fireworks outside the Coach and I would like to know who paid for them. Perhaps some decent citizen was trying to blow the place up and Norman mistook the action for a party.

But I had something of a small and private party myself before I set out for Lambourn. The great man came over unexpectedly from Antibes on business and he invited me to the Ritz for a drink. He brought me a load of the very good vitamins he takes and which he says will give me the courage to go on. It isn't very often that you meet someone you admire tremendously who turns out to be as nice as you would have hoped for them to be. Mr Greene is aces. But what a strange hotel the Ritz is. They took half an hour to bring up some soda water. Are they employing Norman's rejects?

So the past few days have been a little hectic and the body is screaming for a rest but the trouble with an old banger is that if you switch the engine off you might not be able to start it again. But GG's vitamins are mustard. They have caffeine in them and they rev me up in the morning. Just as well because I have another date in Lambourn in a few days' time. The trainers and jockeys are giving a do. I shall take some extra ice cubes for the nostrils. I just don't know how they do it. I suppose if you ride out every day at dawn you get to be fit enough for any sort of battle. Taxis don't do it for me.

Angry Young Man *8 October 1988*

I had a very unpleasant experience in the pub last Sunday. I was sitting at the bar having a drink with Pickles when a lager yob, dressed in a leather jacket decorated with badges, walked up to me and snarled, 'Allo, boy. You're an old man. You haven't got long to live so why don't you sod off now?' How does such spontaneous hate and anger come about? Why did he pick on me, a total stranger, as the object of his verbal violence? I know I look like an old man and I know that it is very probable and likely that I will die in a twinkling of God's eye. So what? I am just puzzled as to what emotional nerve the sight of me struck in that young man. You think I am getting soft? Don't you believe it. What I am getting is depressed at the lack of kindness about these days. If I had kept my eyes open I could have diagnosed this cancer of the heart and soul in the 1960s. Even so there was nothing we could have done to stop the growth.

So what else is new? Well, they have put ham, mash and haricot beans on the menu in the Groucho Club and jolly good it is too. Such is the headline news I have for you this week. Turning to the inside pages I see that nobody wept into their whisky tumblers last week and that the defeat of Unfuwain in the Arc de Triomphe hit some people where it can really hurt.

But to go back to that nasty young man. I am trying to remember what made me so disgustingly aggressive when I was his age. Lack of self-esteem probably, which could have been cured by an injection of money. I also used to break my knuckles hitting inanimate objects. Frustration, I suppose, which could have been cured by a few more leg-overs. The last inanimate object I hit was Graham Mason. But anger is ebbing, thank God. It is very difficult to lose your temper if you are so clapped out that you can't get out of bed until it is opening time. Anger, like hate, requires a lot of energy and I think it may have dietary roots and quite subtle ones. Chinamen blow their stacks at the drop of a hat but the hot spice-eating Thais are as bland as mud. And, dear oh dear, don't I know some angry women. If Ernest Hemingway were alive today I could introduce him to a few of them who would prompt him to write *Tea in the Afternoon*.

Now that the pubs are open all day I have noticed that people are having rows much earlier in the day. I recorded a 'you make me sick' of seven on the Richter scale as early as 4 p.m. last Monday. In effect the new drinking law has put the clocks forward by four hours. Married couples used not to attempt soul murder until they got home. Now it's a public daylight job. There is a couple who come into the pub who are destined to play to 'packed houses' as a theatre critic would say.

Anyway, to change the subject. I think you ought to know that there is a fishmonger round the corner from where I live who is so daft and stupid that he has actually put up a notice in the window of his shop which says, 'Closed owing to illness'. Now I know how the word salmonella was derived. Most of the shopkeepers and publicans around here are mad. There is one man who keeps telling me that he is all alone in his shop and that he has got ever so much money in the till. I don't know whether he wants to perpetrate an inside job with me and go 50–50 or whether he has a longing to see me banged up in the nick for a few months. A female publican asked me the other night if I would stand up and lend her my stool so that she could hit her husband with it. (I told her that if I could stand up I would be home in bed.) A nutcase of an Indian said, 'Please pay me when it suits you. I have seen your picture in the paper', when I went in for a lousy pint of milk. And there is a completely paranoid Italian who has a restaurant that is always completely empty. He insists that every single table has been reserved and you can't even smell the odour of cooking in the place. No, there's more to Covent Garden than the Royal Opera House and I hope I don't catch it. And now I must go to the pub to get my daily dose of injustice.

Curse of the Sausage Roll

15 October 1988

I bought a woman a drink yesterday. Ten minutes later I bought her another one. A further ten minutes after that she bought herself one. Just herself. Equality? I make that little session a 3–0 win. Feminists never realize just how much the majority of women welcome, like and need male chauvinist pigs. She has a job too and doesn't have to walk the tightrope that is the freelancer's conductor and earth. You could buy drinks all day for people who are flat broke but to hell with people like that. It was like finding that the milk has turned sour.

A trivial incident? No, not at all. When I was a barman for a while 25 years ago it always fascinated me to watch a man who could outfumble his friends for an entire session. An Ascot Gold Cup winner. A real stayer. A man, as the cockneys say, who could peel an orange in his pocket. Oh well, it takes all sorts and what a bloody shame that is. I knew a man once who damn nigh destroyed himself through a petty act of meanness. He pinched a sausage roll from the buffet on Paddington Station, got nicked and was thenceforth known to everyone as 'the sausage bandit'. After a while people couldn't remember his proper name. He was a film extra when I was a clapper boy on one of the greatest films of all time called *Zarak Khan*, which starred Victor Mature, Anita Ekberg and Michael Wilding. Nic Roeg was the camera operator. When they wanted the said extra in shot the assistant director would shout, 'Bring on the sausage bandit.'

What strange days they were. There was another awful film on which Martita Hunt asked me to sit on her lap between takes. It was probably that that made me flee to the cutting rooms and become an assistant editor. She used to stroke me and say, 'I want to buy you lots of pretty jerseys.' She never did. But Anita Ekberg was something else, as they say. I have never been obsessed like most men about women's breasts but hers were quite extraordinary and had electricians almost falling off the gantry to get a closer look. She didn't need a bra, she needed scaffolding. Actually she didn't. Her breasts were quite capable of making their own arrangements. I find it quite amazing today to think that there was a time when the sight of a woman as stunning as Ekberg could make me *itch*.

Ingrid Bergman was a lovely person. I worked on *Anastasia* and apart from the ubiquitous sausage bandit there was the dreaded Yul Brynner. Not nice. The best bunch of people were on *The Guns of Navarone*. It wasn't a bad job either what with alternating lunch breaks between the studio bar and The Ship in Shepperton. On a good week and with a bit of overtime I earned £35. *Mais pas de* sausage bandit. The last time I saw him was on a dreadful pilot for a television series which never got made but which starred Donald Wolfit. (By this time Nic Roeg was lighting cameraman.) That was at Nettlefold Studios at Walton-on-Thames. Wolfit struck me as being one of the greatest hams of all time, on a par with Anthony Quinn.

Of course, what annoyed me about those days, frustrated me anyway, was the fact that being an assistant editor made it very improbable that I could get a budding starlet to bed. Others had their evil way but I sulked in the pub. Then in 1962 I got a job in the cutting rooms at Ealing Studios working for the BBC. I wouldn't want to work for that organization again. Actually, to call it an organization is to flatter it. Never have I come into contact with so many madmen and women. We made a documentary called *The Death Penalty* and had Albert Pierrepoint in the studio for three days. A rum cove. He really had enjoyed being the public hangman. (Could you be a private hangman?) It gave me the creeps sometimes to listen to him talking as we sat in the canteen. With him about wild horses couldn't have dragged me to the pub. I asked him once was it true that the prisoner always ate a hearty breakfast? He said, 'I'm not sure but I always did.' Ho, ho. I suppose he would have hanged the sausage bandit had he been on that film. Such a mild little chap was Albert. I'm told Himmler was too. Well, if they bring it back it's a job that Norman could do.

Silver Spoon Wanted

29 October 1988

I telephoned Newmarket last night and all is well for the time being. The Inland Revenue, though, are lurking in the wings and for that matter I think I can hear them coming up my stairs. All these people – tax, VAT, Customs and Excise – are relentless. They won't let go, like dogs with bones. Two years ago the Customs and Excise had me arrested. A few weeks ago, they asked me to an office party. Why? And now the Coach and Horses is crawling with CID people. It probably always has been. I can't see their fascination in the place. It is just a kennel to this dog and all the customers are harmless, except to themselves, of course.

This is nothing new to me. There was a prefect at school – he should have been called Jouvet – who spent two years in the hope of catching me smoking. He used to pop up everywhere. In the bicycle shed, into my hut in the woods and he often searched my desk and bed as though I was daft enough to keep cigarettes there. Then he would stop me to smell my breath for the tell-tale nicotine. He eventually got me for telling one boy to 'f——— off' and I suppose he is probably a detective-inspector now. We will meet again no doubt when the ridiculous Edwina Currie makes it a criminal offence to smoke. Oh, *and* drink. Mind you, I once had to dispense with a literary agent because she drank too much. She was very surprised but I pointed out to her, quite logically I thought, that one of us had to be sober and it certainly wasn't going to be me.

Anyway, the Inland Revenue, it would seem, want a little more than £1 million from Lester. He should seek advice from Lord Vestey, an expert in tax matters. Otherwise he might end up having to dip into his Bahamas number four account. But it isn't disaster. As Lord Howard de Walden once said, 'One million is very like another million.' How true. Oddly enough Lord Howard was my landlord once. I met him at Newbury races one day long ago and asked him for a rent reduction. He was quite taken aback and obviously didn't realize that I was pulling his leg. He advised me to speak to his agent. I suppose it must make a man feel pretty safe to own practically everything between Baker Street and Great Portland Street. Owning a Derby winner must be fairly encouraging too.

I have often wondered what the odds are against being born of a duke and duchess. Given Debrett's and the figure of the population I suppose it would be easy enough to work out. But I do think it is a little unfair to be a skint mister. It isn't a very tidy life from where I am sitting although She who has abandoned the ironing board very kindly cleared away the spilt cottage pie from the carpet yesterday. It had been there for three days, dried out a bit and came away in her gracious hand quite easily. No, I don't think that Lord Howard de Walden need concern himself with the right-hand column, the prices, of a menu. He would make a suitable father never mind a duke.

I mention the business of menus because these petty considerations are not heeded by Waldens or dukes. Eating so many meals out is a financial killer. It is not my idea of bliss to sit here alone in the dark of the night trying to eat cottage pie bought for me by Norman. So the restaurant bills are piling up and I think that this room is being bugged by various authorities. It's a mess. Very different from life at Chatsworth I would say. The fuchsia is dying in the soda water and the overflow pipe from the fourth floor of the genito-urinary hospital doesn't stop spewing forth and keeping me awake all night. I have run out of tea-bags and there is only an inch of vodka left in the bottle.

Reading the label on that bottle I see that Pierre Smirnoff ceased purveying vodka to the Czars in 1917. One can only wonder why. And now it is back to M & S for some more cottage pie and tonight we shall attempt to eat it from a plate. Not the family plate though.

Out in the Cold

5 November 1988

Many, many years ago, I spent an afternoon making love to a rather silly woman who was married to a Member of Parliament. Labour, of course. She was so daftly innocent in her way that during the overture she said, 'But we can't do this in the afternoon. People don't make love in daylight, do they?' Fearful that her frenzy would evaporate and be distilled into afternoon tea and conversation I reassured her saying, 'It's quite all right. They've put the clocks back.' That made it acceptable.

I am reminded of that afternoon because it is so cold and winter is with us again. On that occasion it was so cold that I had to soak for 20 minutes in a hot bath before overture and beginners. I have been colder, though, and the coldest was at the original Outward Bound, based at Aberdovey. That was November too. They woke us up at 5.30 a.m. and then we went for a two-mile run. Okay. But after that we had to have a cold shower. Those showers were so cold that they actually winded us. They took your breath away. We were more or less held under them for 30 seconds and there was no life until some porridge later. It was also nigh freezing sailing whalers in an angry Cardigan Bay. What a place. If it takes that sort of place to make a man of you I would rather be a woman. The afternoons were devoted to sport, and jumping hurdles we slipped on the ice and our javelins skidded over the frost. Some mothers will do anything to get rid of a son for a while.

So cold that it was physically painful was New York City in November 1970. The streets and avenues were littered with broken umbrellas ripped out of their owners' hands by the icy wind. I had no overcoat or the money with which to buy one and I was desperate. Then, by chance, I bumped into Francis Bacon who saved the day and not for the first or last time. Breakfasts of Dom Perignon in the Algonquin every morning for a while and an overcoat followed. I also met a hot-water bottle in the shape of a friendly woman who had the strange name of Ricki Rheingold. A terrible winter that.

There was a cold winter that I did enjoy though. Phillip O'Connor, the author of a weird and fascinating autobiography, *Public Baby*, lent me a cottage in Suffolk and I got a job from the neighbouring farmer. For two months I worked at hedging and ditching and it was tremendously satisfying. It was marvellous to make a stretch of hedge and a ditch clean, nice and tidy. After every 20 yards or so I made a little bonfire with what I had cut and sat down and had some tea from the thermos. The country was crystal clear. Cloudless pale-blue skies and the cold brought everything into the sharpest of focuses so that a frozen blade of grass was as a needle. Blackbirds and squirrels followed my progress along the edges of the frozen meadows, and then just as I was beginning to feel like St Francis of Assisi the spell was broken.

One night, sipping my lamb stew in the ingle-nook, it occurred to me to ask Robert Colquhoun and Robert McBryde to come and stay for a couple of weeks. Mistake, much as I loved them. They drank too much and in those days I thought drink was for Saturday nights. Beer only too. Well, I kept the lamb stew going, adding to it for an age while they had rows. McBryde got hysterical making bad jokes about the atom bomb which he called the autumn bum and I got so fed up with Colquhoun one night I kicked him into a ditch. I felt rotten about that. He was a very good man indeed. Anyway, in those days it only took two weeks for the Roberts to make their impression on everyone wherever they happened to be and the farmer gave us our marching orders. I have never liked work very much but I handed in my pitchfork and sickle with great reluctance. No more log fires, bonfires and blackbirds eating the crusts of my sandwiches under the frozen blue silence of that sky. I could have killed them but they managed that themselves in their own good time. I miss them a lot.

And now another winter of our discontent has begun. The electric fire and the posh meals are no substitute for the lamb stew taken in the ingle-nook. I mean it.

Dead End

19 November 1988

How I wish life was like playing in repertory. Sadly, it isn't. I feel as though I have had a walk-on part in, say, *The Mousetrap* ever since its first night: 56 years of asking, 'Anyone for tennis?' and getting no reply. Even my doubles partners have all walked out on me. Never mind.

Well, I do actually. I lay awake for hours last night trying to work out whether it might be possible to change life. I don't think it is. It takes a supertanker something like 20 miles to stop, I'm told, and even this dinghy can't change course. I often think of making a geographical change but in my experience it just does not work. If you went to the South Pole the first person you would meet there would be yourself. Short bursts of travel can alleviate the pain but in the end life is terminal. What I hate is that I know *exactly* how the rest of today is going to go. It is too late to become a merchant banker. Unable to cope with my insights into the human condition I shall go to the pub shortly. A man came in there recently and started to chat to me. He told me that he was an English teacher and went on to say that the trouble with this column is that it is full of self-pity. How very wrong. I haven't felt sorry for myself for at least ten years. I think it is all a hoot and at the very least I am trudging to the grave with a wry smile.

So how to change it all? I suppose I could start going to the Carlisle Arms instead of the Coach and Horses. Switch from vodka to gin. A whole new world might open up. You know how it is when a train is travelling between railway embankments and you get impatient for a view? Well, that's how it is. I believe there is a foreign trip in the offing so that might get rid of a few days, which is an awful way to think, as though one's days were like money burning a hole in one's pocket. The thing is I am so short of a challenge – waking up in the morning is too easy – I might have to take drastic steps and either get married again or have both my legs amputated. Something decisive anyway.

So what else is on the agenda? Well, I went to buy the microwave last week, had its workings demonstrated to me and was suddenly overcome with extreme feelings of stinginess. I am now going to buy a bedside refrigerator instead. Ice is essential and waking up in the morning to sour milk is symptomatic of decline in the way that hanging one's clothes on the floor and not bothering to shave is. It should be possible to plan things so that it would not be necessary to have to get out of bed ever again. The fact that I am beginning to look like Edith Sitwell would lend a touch of credence to that state of apathy as well.

Norman telephoned the pub from hospital yesterday and asked me to give him a report on the behaviour of his regulars. I was able to tell him that his ship was still on course and that we are all still spending as much money as possible reserving only enough for a biscuit and glass of milk last thing at night. He then somewhat amazed me by saying, 'If you need any money just help yourself.' The poor man is still hiccuping and I think that may be worse than having a bad back. He keeps putting the back out again and again when he suddenly sits up in bed to scream at his wife. She really should stop visiting him but she actually loves him. So, you see, it's true. There is someone for everyone. Even Hitler had his Eva but I don't suppose that visiting him in hospital after the bomb plot could have been any worse than visiting Norman with hiccups. The doctors should stop messing about and simply give him the fright of his life. News of financial disaster would put him on his feet again. How awful to think that we need the bastard. A really nice bloke behind that bar would be unthinkable.

Go East, Young Woman

26 November 1988

My daughter is going to Australia today and I wonder if she will ever come back. I advised her to stay for keeps if she likes it and is happy there, for there isn't much here. She will probably end up with a lifeguard on Bondi Beach. A couple of years ago, attempting to ascertain whether or not history was still taught in schools, I asked her who succeeded Lenin and she told me Stanley Baldwin. Apart from anything else what are the odds against a Russian being called by the awful name of Stanley? And her school chum thought that Magna Carta was King John's wife. I can go along with that. I have met a lot of overbearing women like hospital matrons who could have well been called Magna, but Stanley Baldwin knocked me sideways.

Is there hope for such a girl? Only if she is very pretty and funny. She is. What I fear, though, is that her addiction to pop music will lead her to a mindless young man. I would like to wash my hands of it all but of course I can't. She also has the strange notion that because people say hallo to me in Old Compton Street or Dean Street I am rich. She should know by now that the only people who are rich are those who work in advertising or those who have inherited the stuff. So, it's bye-bye Isabel and don't forget to write. Brush your teeth, take the pill and don't follow beaten favourites in two-year-old races. What else can you tell a girl? Damned if I know. Anyway, I am glad she didn't turn out to be a boy. Nasty little things mostly until they are about 30.

Oh that I could be 18 and setting out for pastures new. Who knows, there might be a boy in Sydney today who is setting out for Soho, London, England. Silly sod. Stay put. If Harold Larwood settled there it can't be bad. It gets worse here by the minute. Too many people have died for my liking. I see faces in my mind's eye – gone forever – that I would love to see walk into the Coach and Horses today. Yesterday I saw a man put out his cigarette on the carpet. That says it all. Most of it anyway. What says it here is that I woke up with a chicken bone on the pillow this morning. Other signs of decline and decay are wearing the same pair of socks for two days running and allowing a pat of butter to melt on my pocket calculator. The fact that I have nothing to calculate is neither here nor there.

Maybe the worst indication of a sort of decline, though, is the business of talking to idiots. I hate unsolicited chat in bars – it can occasionally be interesting on trains – but once a man starts by telling me that it is raining or that flogging is too good for football hooligans then I am drawn in and can linger prattling for an age. It is odd that every single stranger who comes into the pub knows just what is best for the country. The idea of the reintroduction of National Service is a favourite topic at the moment. The quickly disappearing rain forests of Brazil is second and permanently on the chart is the matter of the Booker Prize. Most boring of all is a racing man's post-mortems. I am sure we didn't talk like that in Soho pubs 30 years ago but I suspect we talked about money too much, the obsession of writers, poets and painters.

But the smell of burning feathers in the Coach and Horses is awful because we rise every morning like so many phoenixes. You see people walk in like beaten boxers coming out of their corner very gamely for the last round. Norman, the referee, should have stopped a lot of these metaphorical fights to have saved us from further punishment. He, by the way, has discharged himself from the Middlesex Hospital and moved into a very expensive nursing home. I shouldn't be surprised if he moves into Buckingham Palace soon. He knows how to take care of himself does our Norman. He mollycoddles himself and even has his hair cut once a week. Whether he likes the sensation or whether it gives him an opportunity to look into a mirror for half an hour without seeming to be vain I know not.

Still, I suppose looking after yourself like he does is better than wearing the same pair of socks for two days running and leaving chicken bones in the bed.

Who's Coming to Dinner?

10 December 1988

A magazine has asked me to name my six favourite and six unfavourite people of all time. Sixty would have been easier but just six is hard. Too many people have to be left out. It would have been all too easy to name the likes of Pinochet, Amin and Khomeini in the shit list but I thought that would have been a little dull. Oddly enough I couldn't think of one woman to put on the list of favourites but Joan of Arc immediately came to mind when I began to think of unfavourites. Were she alive today I am pretty sure she would be living in either Hackney or Islington, subscribing to the *Guardian* and being a one-parent, militant lesbian family woman. Unless she was a boy in drag, that is. She was closely followed by Napoleon, the man who stamped all over Europe and killed thousands of people. Never trust a man with a small member.

As well as dictators I thought I would exclude members of the Nazi party as being a little too obvious and I certainly couldn't have put Goering on the list since he would have had the good sense to blow up the Arts Council. It was easier to kick off with the list of favourites. Readers of this column will not be surprised that Byron sprang to mind. A kind and humane man I would have liked to have dined with at least once a week for a lifetime. Holland House in the evenings. What days!

I have to include Nelson who, with all his sillinesses and vanity, is *the* hero. Most people get him a little wrong. He was ruthless and didn't just want to beat the French, he wanted to annihilate them. Pity he didn't. I had wanted to include Nye Bevan on the list but I had to pass him over for Fred Astaire who made envy legitimate. You wouldn't have minded being in his shoes, so to speak. And Charles Dickens would have been entirely welcome to this wretched typewriter, the feckless Monica. I gather he was a difficult man. So what? Biographies and dramas are not the gospel and I regard the play *Amadeus* as not much more than a curiosity. It matters not one jot whether Mozart was anally fixated. Anyway, he would have made a fart sound divine. So he can come to dinner.

Washing up dishes in the kitchen with Joan of Arc and Napoleon I see the dreaded Jeremy Thorpe putting the left-over scraps in the dustbins and so doing something useful. He is not to be allowed a doggy bag. Oh, that ridiculous hat and those silly waistcoats. What a lucky man: I wish I could come up in front of deranged magistrates and judges. Deranged in my favour, that is. The Ulster quack Ian Paisley is in there too, hopefully putting the oven to use by putting his head in it while the cheese is being served. But, as I say, these lists are over-subscribed.

Just to get drunk with I would have liked Ulysses S. Grant to come along with his boss Lincoln. Yes, 60 likes and dislikes would have been a lot easier to choose than six. I would have taken the risk of inviting J. M. W. Turner. As far as I can see no one seems to know much about the *man*. After this celestial dinner it would have been good to have a game of backgammon with Charles James Fox, one of the great punters in our country's history. Norman, by the way, has been under the table for the duration of this repast clearing up the breadcrumbs. But he does get a pat on the head as well as being blamed by all for Mozart's farts. His is truly a dog's life. There has to be a place too by the kitchen sink for Derek Jameson. He definitely belongs downstairs with Elastoplast across his mouth.

And it is downstairs in the kitchen that the housekeeper Margaret Thatcher runs a tight ship. Starched from head to toe, she gives Napoleon a clip across the ear every time she passes him. Just for luck, she says. And now, with no ladies present, we can smoke, although it is rumoured that Maria Callas is to make a guest appearance accompanied at the piano by Chopin. They can hear her downstairs as they howl with hunger and lick the dirty plates. Grant mistakes Norman's head for an ashtray and stubs a cigar out on him. Fox is writing me out an IOU and Dickens is taking copious notes. It is with great relief that I know for a certainty that I am going to heaven and not downstairs. Put out the candles, Norman, and let Mozart loose with a lullaby.

Big Bad Woolf

14 January 1989

A strange thing happened last Thursday evening. When I got home and closed the front door behind me, I had a sudden pain in my chest as though I had been kicked by a cart-horse and I fell to the floor. The next thing I remember was lying on a table in the casualty department of University College Hospital. By that time the pain had radiated to my left shoulder and I thought here we go and I haven't even made out a will. I had particularly wanted to leave 14 compact discs to She who would once iron 14 shirts for me. So I lay there dreading heaven and desperately trying to think of some famous and witty last words when they gave me a pain-killing injection and I drifted off.

When I came to, She was sitting there next to me. It's a funny thing but some women – no, most of them – look at you reproachfully even if you have been knocked down by a truck. 'Now look at what you've gone and done to that truck,' sort of thing. Just as I was about to excuse my smoking and drinking to her they slapped an oxygen mask over my face, thus preventing me uttering my famous last words which were going to be, 'Could you please sew some new buttons on the blue and white checked shirt?'

After a while they carted me off to the casualty ward. It was a mixed ward. In there they gave me some tranquillizers to prevent nasty withdrawal symptoms from the Coach and Horses, Groucho Club and Muthaiga Club and I was then at peace. Unfortunately a woman opposite me woke me up in the middle of the night by repeatedly moaning, 'Percy, Percy.' I didn't think that they still called people Percy although I am aware that the Australians call the penis Percy. The woman, though, did not moan with an Australian accent. But she went on and on and I couldn't sleep any more.

By breakfast time the pain had gone and I felt in very good nick and ready for a day on the town. They gave me a boiled egg for breakfast which doesn't say much for the dreaded Edwina Currie and it has yet to strike me down. Then it was chest X-ray time and after that the nurses surprised me by allowing me to smoke a cigarette. Never have I come across such nice nurses and I have met many. In the sober light of day the sight of the woman who had been calling for Percy was rather depressing. But I suppose you have to admire the bravery of a woman of 70 who will wear a see-through nightie.

In the middle of the morning the consultant and his team came to my bedside. He said, 'I'm afraid you have me beaten, Mr Bernard. I can't see anything wrong with you.' I thought this must be the first truly honest doctor I have come across. They can nearly always see something wrong with you, indeed if they couldn't they would all be out of work. After an amazing lunch of minced beef, mash and peas they let me go. I went immediately to the Coach and Horses for a drink and to milk some sympathy from Norman. When I told him what had happened the cold-hearted bastard just said, 'Oh, I thought you'd been drinking in another pub.' When I eventually got home I got even less sympathy. My landlady who had summoned the ambulance said, 'I was terrified you were going to die and that I would have to clear your room up.' She didn't even bother to telephone me so I shall cut her out of any future will and say my famous last words to a stranger or Percy's bride should we meet again in casualty.

Before I left the hospital they showed me the X-ray of my chest and it would seem that my heart has never been broken. Odd. I could have sworn it had. Were all those tears just to wash the eyeballs? Apparently. Anyway, since that 'kick' in the chest various cracker-barrel philosophers – Soho abounds with them – have told me to regard it as warning from on high to ease up. I'll drink to that.

And now I think I am ill again. Last night I dreamt that I woke up in bed one morning and found Virginia Woolf lying beside me. I am no stranger to nightmares but that shattered me. And dreams often reflect the chemistry of the body. But, as Richard West commented, it could have been worse. It could have been Andrea Dworkin. You simply daren't close your eyes nowadays for fear of dreaming or your heart stopping with a bang.

That Strain Again *21 January 1989*

So much music evokes so many places, times and people for me. It can be all sorts of music. My last wife was the Sibelius Symphony No 1, and an awful bit of pop called 'How Much Is That Doggie In The Window' was at the top of the charts when Stanley Matthews was playing for Stoke City and I was working there in the mines. That was in 1952. The Bach Brandenburg Concerto No 3 always takes me back to prep. school and the first woman I ever fancied, who was a young schoolmistress who played a piano arrangement of it. I can still see her legs and heaven knows I spent enough time trying to look up them. That boring man César Franck was with me for weeks when I first left home and got an awful bedsitter in South Ken. And so on.

The other night I played a compact disc of Haydn's Quartet No 1 Op. 20 and it took me right back to Chelsworth and I was awake all night remembering that. What an odd village it was. It was divided into two parts, not physically or geographically, but by class. I called my end the broad bean end and the other the roses end. It was reputedly one of the prettiest villages in England and there were times when I thought it was a little too pretty. We had a thatched cottage with no amenities – no bathroom, that is – and a small garden with an outside lavatory at the end of it. The rent was 3/6d a week but we still struggled a little on my £15 a week from *Town* Magazine. At first we were on the Sunday morning cocktail party list but we gradually got struck off. First by the vicar because I pissed in his garden and then, far worse, by the local bigwig for asking for a refill of Tio Pepe instead of waiting to be offered one.

What I did enjoy was being captain of the village cricket team, drinking all day in Sudbury with Maurice Richardson on market days and sipping whisky in the winter evenings by the fireside in the Peacock and listening to two farm labourer friends talking absolute rubbish. You know the sort of thing: if a thrush shits on you before midday then it will rain for a year. Our next-door neighbour was a nasty old bird who looked like the witch in *Snow White* and I took secret revenge on her by creeping into her garden in the middle of the night, digging a hole in it and then emptying our Elsan bucket into it. And she thought she was a good gardener.

But the thing I thought mostly about during this sleepless night of remembrance was walking my dog Smedley at dusk on autumn and winter evenings. She was a very pale Labrador bitch – the pallor native to East Anglia – and she was one of the kindest souls ever. I had a very good gun, a Cogswell & Harrison, and when the sun began to dip below the trees of the wood we would walk along through the mist that gathered above and beside the river. She would go along ahead of me, stopping from time to time to look back and see if I was still following, and I would be looking out and listening for pheasants, wood pigeons and rabbits. I was poaching but I couldn't feel too bad about it for the farmer didn't spend money on breeding game. It was just there, like the trees that had been there for hundreds of years. An all too rare treat we had was to see the barn owl gliding down along the river. He was so powerful that one languid flap of his great wings would carry him about a hundred yards. Freewheeling majesty. Then, when the sun had really sunk, we walked home through the wet grass, the smell of gunpowder lingering, cold and hungry towards the log fire.

I remember my wife cooking great fish pies with cheese sauce topping and we ate them by the fire while Smedley stared into the flames. I used to wonder what a dog could be thinking about so hard. How odd that Haydn should remind me of all that. I think Haydn would be a good name for a dog. Anyway, it may have been the broad bean end of the village but we had honeysuckle around the door. I also had a garden shed in which I was going to write the novel of the century. What came between us? The bees don't buzz quite like they used to. And now there is a giant pneumatic drill in the street outside and they are making a lot of noise behind me repairing the walls of the genito-urinary hospital. It is too much. I shall put on the Haydn again and go back to Chelsworth and raise a glass to Smedley.

Future Shock

4 February 1989

Death is no longer number one on my chart of private fears. It has been replaced by an outsider called The Possible Danger of Living Too Long. Apart from the fact that London along with most of the rest of the world has become quite disgusting, and that I left it about 25 years too late to get a decent flat, I saw the people who will be running this country soon in the Coach and Horses one evening last week. They were sitting on the floor drinking beer out of bottles and cans. They were all tattooed, in need of soap and hot water and very noisy. I told them off although I know I had no right to. I must be getting old or perhaps I'd had too many drops of the old infuriator. So I asked them why they didn't sit at a table or on the barstools and drink out of glasses. I felt suddenly very depressed. I was looking at the thin end of a revolting wedge.

At least none of them offered to hit me, but I am past caring about that sort of nonsense now, anyway. No, I wouldn't care to be sitting on a park bench and reminiscing 15 years from now. Oh for a time machine and to have been born in either 1770 or 1850. Any further back than that and the troubadors must have been as awful as Muzak. And jousting probably attracted hooligans. Give me the champagne louts of yesteryear. It is a pretty bleak view from the window of my head. The only alternative I can see to being ruled by lager addicts sitting on the chewing gum-encrusted floor is being governed by Camden feminist lesbians. Even Arthur Scargill or Norman would be preferable.

On the credit side of this thing called life is the fact that I am off to Australia next week. Only for two weeks but it will be a breath of fresh air. And I stop off on the way to inspect Singapore. That is a place I particularly look forward to eating in. I look forward to seeing Isabel, my daughter, and I will look up Harold Larwood if he still lives in Sydney. (It was a great mistake to drop him. England needs him now even if he is 80-something.)

As a warm-up, a pipe-opener, for this gruesome journey I

am going to Norwich today to have supper with my favourite poet, George Barker. It was George who reintroduced me to poetry when I was 18 years old, having hated it at school where I was made to learn pages of Keats by heart. (Why have they never forced children to learn *prose* by heart?) The reintroduction was via Ezra Pound of all people. We struck up a correspondence when he was in St Elizabeth's Hospital in Washington. Some bastard subsequently stole the letters from Pound and sold them but I remember him going on and on about how I should keep reading the dictionary. How right he was. On every page of Jonathan Meades's excellent new book, *Peter Knows What Dick Likes*, there is a word that has me groping for the dictionary. That alone makes 597 words that I do not know the meaning of. A bad education sticks to you like marmalade to the carpet.

Yes, it's infectious. Here am I criticizing soul murder by chewing gum and lager and I am typing in a pool of Tiptree Old Times marmalade and Cossack vodka. Had I been writing this column when I was ten it would have been lemon curd and sherbert. You can spot a lout in the nursery. When I was seven the girl next door used to ask me to come and see her in her bath at bedtime. Bathsheba? I would very much like to know what she is doing now. Probably subbing on the *Sun*. Maybe sobbing on a sofa. And talking of tears, the Coach and Horses is now awash with them every night. Two discontented women cry from 8 p.m. until closing time. It is undignified and tiresome and makes it quite pointless for them to put on make-up before venturing forth in search of Mr Wrong.

God, they look a sight when the taps have been running for half an hour or so. Like a loss of sweat I should think a loss of tears on that scale should require salt tablets. Thank heaven my well has dried up. The only thing that could make me cry now would be for me to find the daughter drinking lager, chewing gum and weeping in a bar in Sydney next week. Until then I shall ponder whether or not Hitler spread the carpets he chewed with marmalade.

Man's Worst Friend

11 February 1989

The journey by rail from Norwich to Liverpool Street last Sunday night was a nightmare. The first leg of the trip was a two-carriage job to Ipswich. From there we travelled by bus to Colchester. From where I was sitting on the top deck I got the impression that the driver was drunk. At Colchester we were directed to the wrong platform three times and I thought these legs of mine would give in. It then took nearly two hours of stopping, starting and then crawling into London. The buffet was closed. I would have given a fiver for a cup of tea, never mind a drink.

But it was my companion on this third leg of the journey that made me so anxious to get home. Lying on the floor next to me was a bloody great Doberman Pinscher belonging to the attractive woman sitting opposite. The Doberman didn't bite me but the mere presence and close proximity of the beast was unnerving. And the presence of a Doberman is not mere. I never forget that they were bred for killing people and I almost accidentally stubbed a cigarette out on it. I thought its owner would address it as Fang but she kept calling it Sweetie. I read once that three Dobermans owned by a security company were being exercised in Hyde Park and when they got off their lead they attacked an old woman sitting on a bench and ate her. I kept thinking of that while Sweetie sat next to me on the train.

And now I face another horrendous journey, although there will be no Dobermans but a drinks buffet. By the time you read this I will have been sitting on an aeroplane for 12 hours. I am dreading it. I can't sleep on aeroplanes and I very much dislike using alcohol as a general anaesthetic. In the normal course of events it is merely a local one. In the light of recent disasters I am no longer nervous of flying. I am downright frightened. What assurances do we who are Singapore- and Sydney-bound have that there are no Aboriginal separatists working as luggage handlers? I would prefer to save myself for a funnel-web spider.

I gather that after you have been bitten by one you have a full 20 minutes in which to reflect on your past follies. It isn't quite long enough to cram them all in but it is better than nothing.

Given happy landings at the end of the first stage of the trip, I look forward to following Frances Bissell's advice. She writes the cookery column for the *Times* and I believe she has aimed me in the right direction, so I shall call in at Hsieh's Garden restaurant. I like very much the sound of deep-fried chicken which has been marinated for a day in ginger, honey, spring onions and salt and pepper. Then there is always clay-pot lobster and roast pigeon. Come two weeks' time it will be back to Marks & Sparks takeaways.

Speaking of which, some members of the staff in the Coach and Horses are quite daft. One of the barmen did some shopping there and brought me back a shepherd's pie not much bigger than a postage stamp plus a carton of cauliflower cheese enough to serve four. It was the equivalent of serving a man 6lb of potatoes accompanied by a single sausage. They don't think, you see. The lower the IQ of a man the more likely he will be able to get a job in that pub. I think that maybe unconsciously it is Norman's way of telling us that he despises us for drinking.

And now the telephone has just rung and a magazine has asked me to try and pick up a woman in Sydney and write about it. Well, it could be fun but I am a little out of practice. And I should have asked for some advance expenses. Pulling people always involves expenditure. Years ago, when Harold Evans was editor of the *Sunday Times*, he gave me the money to write about spending a night with an upmarket call girl. I settled for a short time and spent the remaining cash on an excellent dinner and wine. I did the right thing.

Wish You Were Here . . .

25 February 1989

Sydney

Singapore, the stop-off on the way to Sydney, was a disappointment. The great Japanese-financed consumer society – thousands of shops overflowing with electronic toys and gadgets, a police state and a high-rise city of architectural monotony – is just about saved by a few good restaurants and the odd colonial house that the Japs missed in the war. I was not sorry to leave the place and I wish I had had the physical fortitude to have gone right on to Sydney in one go. That was another seven hours on and I collapsed on arrival. Not jet lag but something I must have picked up in Singapore. (That's why I didn't get through to you last week.)

It took two days to come back to life and look at Sydney. I like the place and I like the people. I was extremely lucky to be put up in a luxury hotel for the first four days so that bed, room service and a view of the Opera House from the 28th floor gave me time to recover. Of course the place was far too expensive to drink in and I went across the road to a bar called Jackson's which caters for lesser mortals. The first morning I sat there a frail old man joined me at my table on the pavement, sat down with a thump and buried his face in his hands. After a while he looked up at me and said, 'Christ almighty, I haven't been home for five days.' I assumed the poor fellow lived in Melbourne or somewhere in the bush and I asked him where he lived. He raised a weak and trembling hand, leant over to me and pointing to the corner of the block said, 'In that house over there.' I then asked him about his wife. Wouldn't she be worried or angry? No, she would be sitting at home as usual and 'she frightened the dog off his chain last week'. Apparently that meant that she was hideous, not intimidating.

Shortly after that I fell in with a good man, Robert Haupt, from the *Sydney Morning Herald*. His colleagues too are very much okay. He drove me out to Bondi Beach where we had lunch overlooking the whole scene, the Tasman Sea and the beach itself, sitting on a sun-soaked balcony. The beach surprised me, being much smaller than I thought it would be and backed by a built-up area of suburb. There must have been a thousand topless ladies sunbathing and, as has been said, to walk along that beach is like picking your way very carefully through a field of poached eggs. The *Morning Herald* people are very much into playing cards as far as I can tell and trumps last week seemed to be American Express.

On my fifth day here I moved into a hotel called the Palisade. It is a splendid house built in 1915 and the Harbour Bridge is just beyond my balcony where I sit late into the night sipping cocktails to allay the itches inflicted by mosquitoes. It is a well furnished balcony so I sit there and eat takeaway suppers and watch the ships go by as dusk falls. There is another strange hotel around the corner. Strange in so far as the bar opens at 6.30 a.m. and because when I went in there the other evening for a drink the boss said, 'I'm sorry we're late with the fight.' Was there a big fight on television, I asked. No, it was the nightly punch-up they have in the bar. God alone knows how much these fights cost in terms of damages, but they must cost a few bob, the men here being mostly extremely muscular.

I met up with the daughter yesterday and I must say I am a little worried about her. She is happy enough but not working. My own awful upbringing makes me wonder whether she needs a cold shower, a three-mile run and a good thrashing. I certainly didn't get where I am today in Sydney eating oysters and bream and swilling booze by lying in the sun all day. She can have two more lunches and one more hand-out before I leave today and then I shall rinse my hands of her.

And now it is off to the *Sydney Morning Herald* pub for a final game of Barclay Visa cards. By the way, the newsmen here have christened their landlord Norman. You can't escape them. Even from 15,000 miles.

Sprinkler System

11 March 1989

If anyone who had spent their life in an English village, a clearing in a rain-forest, a cave in a mountain or even a lunatic asylum were to walk into the Coach and Horses at any time after 6 p.m. they would be astounded at what they would hear and see. Even frightened. The scene can be quite alarming as well as boring. The bickering, the shouting, the crying, the anger, the abuse and the spite make for a cacophony of Muslim-like intensity. It isn't the moon – we had a new one this week – it could be infected foodstuffs; it isn't the result of unhappy childhoods and I think it may be that alcohol is a little more toxic than I had previously supposed. Or perhaps insanity is contagious.

On top of all that the pub has become deeply attractive to very horrible young people who pack the place so that it is hard to get served never mind throw a drink in a friend's face. But in spite of the simmering violence of a sort, it is the women crying that gets me down the most. I don't mind a teardrop coursing down the channels of a powdered cheek but I draw the line at your actual sobbing at the bar. People should sob into pillows. (What is even worse, though, is to wake up in the middle of the night and to realize that the woman next to you is *silently* crying. That's reproach for you and you just have to get up, go to the kitchen and make some tea.) We have a woman in the pub who howls. A howl is louder than a sob but it is too ridiculous a noise to be touching.

I wonder how all this behaviour would go down in Annabel's or a tough East End pub. Last week a barmaid threw a jug of water over a man because he swore at her. Fair enough. In the East End he probably would have been killed. You have to be awfully careful. Some years ago in the Colony Room Club I told Ronnie Kray not to be such a f———ing bore. I didn't know who he was at the time. But, like all gangsters, he was a bore.

Another thing that happens after six p.m. in the pub is that visiting hooligans drop their chewing gum on the carpet, where it is eventually trodden in by the disgusting hordes. Only Test cricket batsmen facing the quickies should be allowed to chew gum. An ugly habit. I wonder if the women could chew gum and cry at the same time. There was a lovely secretary at the *Daily Mirror* 20 years ago whom I inadvertently made cry quite a lot and she could type letters with tears streaming down her face, although Mike Molloy said she couldn't and would I therefore leave her be. She got married and settled down. Sadly it is a little late for that for the weeping ladies of Soho.

Oddly enough, I have not cried since I *was* married. I admit to some moistness when I last saw *The Railway Children* on television but otherwise I have to keep splashing water on to my face so that I can open and shut the eyes. They are as dry as Islam. Speaking of which, I asked Norman this week to bar Muslims. Before 6 p.m. anyway. He won't and he says he'll take any currency. To be fair, though, I also asked him to bar Rushdie. The fact that the shortly-to-be-smoked Salman is a member of the Groucho Club is causing me grave concern, and I mean grave. I do not want to be blown up while I am toying with my afternoon tea or contemplating the manageress's legs. I have yet to see any women weeping in the Groucho but the time could come.

Blowing up the Coach and Horses would make very little difference to the place. Incendiary devices would be put out by tears anyway. And Norman is probably insured way beyond the hilt. He took his mother out for lunch last Sunday, Mothering Sunday, and apparently she got through five courses, which is not bad for a woman of 93. In fact her age is in dispute. Neither he or she is quite sure how old she is. I suggested to Norman that to cheer her up he should send her a telegram on her next birthday and sign it Elizabeth R. 'Waste of bloody money,' he said. More to the point is that it would probably make her cry.

Living Dangerously *25 March 1989*

I am still sending the food parcels to Salman Rushdie at his secret hideout at 643b Fulham Palace Road, London SW9. It has been a great drain on my slender resources and to have weekly consignments of dates and frozen sheep's eyes specially flown in from Egypt and Morocco is an expensive business, I can tell you. But I would do the same for any hack, millionaire or pauper, whether he or she were being persecuted by the Lord's Day Observance Society, the Inland Revenue, the NUJ or Seventh Day Adventist fanatics. It is bad enough to be spiked by mad editors but to be spiked, as it were, by hordes of lunatic animals must be the last straw for a serious writer.

The trouble is I have other dependants too. Apart from 'Mad' Jock who sleeps beneath the awning of the Palace Theatre and who needs a pint of bitter every day to keep his kidneys in working order, I have just been informed that I have a newish daughter in Bangkok who will need rice, clothes and schooling. Also the rent is due and it was impossible to foresee Beech Road winning the Champion Hurdle at Cheltenham last week. And I am expecting a *cri de coeur* – if not a *cri de poche* – any day now from my daughter in Sydney.

Oh well, we must soldier on. Anyway, Salman is still churning it out. He leaves a chapter a week on the front doorstep and my secret agent, a Unigate milkman, passes it on to me and I then leave it in the Groucho Club for his publisher. I have begun to think that writing is a dangerous business. Those two Camden beauties, Alice Thomas Ellis and Beryl Bainbridge, risk kidnapping by gypsies every time they venture out into the streets. I have had to warn Salman that Ladbrokes are laying 33–1 on him reaching the Muslim-run corner shop in one piece if he sallies forth to buy the *Times Literary Supplement*.

The business of having to lie low must be one hell of a bore and your room would get very stuffy if you didn't dare go to the window to open it for fear of snipers across the road. I daren't open my own modest window because of the air extractor on the wall of the genito-urinary hospital behind me. God knows what germs it is pumping out in my direction. I don't want anything else to go wrong with my genitals. They have already ruined my life.

This is a dangerous place to live. It is a potential fire-trap and now that flat racing is with us again I am more than ever aware of the fact that I live directly over a betting shop. I would even feel safer if it was taken over by Muslims and turned into a mini-market. Oddly enough, I feel slighted in a way at not having been selected by nutcases as an object of persecution, but maybe the anti-smoking loonies and the silly medical profession that wants to keep everyone alive for ever may get around to it. It won't be as dramatic as the case of Salman, though, and I quite like a little drama, especially when it brings in a couple of million pounds. I could write an extremely rude letter to the Ayatollah, I suppose, but since I am convinced that these people can't even read a letter never mind a bestseller of their own making there seems to be little point. Thank God I am incapable of writing a novel. It must be like playing Russian roulette with six bullets in the chamber. Not a bad idea for some.

Ghosts All Around Us. . .

8 April 1989

Wandering about London as I do I find it strange to think of what it must have been like once upon a time. The present is so awful that I am constantly wondering about the past. Perhaps it isn't so strange a thing to think about since we are all surrounded by the past. The nearest pub to where I live is the Cross Keys in Endell Street and struggling to get served in there last night amid a horde of advertising people it occurred to me that Charles Dickens used to drink there. I wondered what he would make of it now. He also drank in the Lamb and Flag off Garrick Street and cars are now double parked where the blacking factory was. Oscar Wilde used to use Kettners long before some idiot introduced the awful pizza to this country. If he went to Kettners fairly frequently it is likely that he had the one in the Coach and Horses opposite.

There are ghosts everywhere and you only have to shut your eyes to see them. The cafés of Paris are jam-packed with them as are the decks of HMS *Victory*. I thought I heard the roar of guns when I walked past them at Vicksburg but the stupid and biased guide brought me down to earth again with her nonsenses. I left the group and walked to a hotel and had a drink with Ulysses Grant. I told him that he had lost at Vicksburg after all and he just shrugged. Back on the paddle steamer Mark Twain steered us safely to Memphis.

But is one perhaps unaware of being surrounded by legends today? Will the walls of the Groucho Club one day be covered with commemorative plaques? I doubt it. I can't think of many people who will be remembered in years to come when those of us alive today have made room at the bar for future generations of advertising executives. I just hope my daughter remembers me. The telephone rang at 6 a.m. this morning and somebody asked me if I would accept a call from Sydney. I knew this was coming. I just knew it. She needs the money to go into hospital to have a couple of wisdom teeth extracted and would I please not be angry and help. I said I wasn't at all angry and okay about the loot. So what else is happening? She is working in a brasserie staffed by gay waiters, has a flat with a friend which they have just painted pink and they have a record player, lots of friends and go out to parties most of the time. It sounds perfectly ghastly to me. Why pink? And I know exactly the sort of records they will be playing.

I am not by nature a suspicious man but I think I will have a look inside her mouth if we meet again to see whether there were offending wisdom teeth in the first place. Not that it matters. I am trying to remember what I was doing when I was 19, that's all. Certainly not painting a flat pink and going to discos with gay waiters. So she also said that I sounded awful and was I ill again? (She is concerned about my health in a horribly matronly way.) I said I was all right but that she had woken me up suddenly. She then asked me three more times was I angry and I told her no. Poor thing. She then said, 'I love you,' and rang off.

What a strange and touching start to the day. An early one too. I went back to bed, dabbed my eyes with Kleenex for Men – that's a joke – and sipped a drink pondering toothache 15,000 miles from home. So the cheque is in the post and all I need to do now is to find the winner of the Grand National and that is a headache if not a toothache. I hate to think what the next telephone call will be about but I think I can guess and I hope he isn't a gay waiter.

Keith Floyd
Floyd in the Soup £4.99

If you can't stand the heat, get out of the kitchen

If Keith Floyd had nurtured any ambition to make money, he would have found himself a proper job. Cooking looked like an easy option . . . until he found himself juggling with three restaurants, a gigantic overdraft and untameable staff.

Something had to give. And throughout his spectacular career it has usually been Keith Floyd. When the bailiffs arrived they wanted everything – including Christmas dinner for 30 at £2.50 a head.

Just when it looked like *out of the frying pan, into the fire,* Floyd was discovered by the Man from the BBC. A debut performance of roast guinea fowl – uniquely stuffed with giblets still in their plastic bag – firmly sealed the flavour of an entertainer whose trademark was chaos in the kitchen.

Since then, fuelled by a love of food and drink, Keith Floyd has shared the cup that cheers with famous and less famous gastronauts – not to mention the millions of viewers of his four BBC TV series.

With this hilarious account of his adventures as a chef, on screen and off, Keith Floyd has prepared the ingredients to perfection, blending scandal and outrage with a lubrication of good spirit that is all his own. FLOYD IN THE SOUP is his unique and spicy creation – lifting the lid off the catering business to reveal the darkest secrets of the kitchen.

All Pan books are available at your local bookshop or newsagent, or can be ordered direct from the publisher. Indicate the number of copies required and fill in the form below.

Send to: **CS Department, Pan Books Ltd., P.O. Box 40, Basingstoke, Hants. RG21 2YT.**

or phone: 0256 469551 (Ansaphone), quoting title, author and Credit Card number.

Please enclose a remittance* to the value of the cover price plus: 60p for the first book plus 30p per copy for each additional book ordered to a maximum charge of £2.40 to cover postage and packing.

*Payment may be made in sterling by UK personal cheque, postal order, sterling draft or international money order, made payable to Pan Books Ltd.

Alternatively by Barclaycard/Access:

Card No. | | | | | | | | | | | | | | | | |

Signature:

Applicable only in the UK and Republic of Ireland.

While every effort is made to keep prices low, it is sometimes necessary to increase prices at short notice. Pan Books reserve the right to show on covers and charge new retail prices which may differ from those advertised in the text or elsewhere.

NAME AND ADDRESS IN BLOCK LETTERS PLEASE:

....

Name ______________________________

Address ______________________________

____

____

____

3/87